Anthology of Contem

GW00890447

Anthology of Contemporary Poetry

Post-war to the Present

Edited by John Wain

Hutchinson of London

Hutchinson & Co. (Publishers) Ltd
3 Fitzroy Square, London W1P 6JD

London Melbourne Sydney Auckland
Wellington Johannesburg and agencies
throughout the world

First published 1979

Set in ACM Century by D.P. Press

Printed in Great Britain by The Anchor Press Ltd
and bound by Wm Brendon & Son Ltd,
both of Tiptree, Essex

British Library Cataloguing in Publication data

Anthology of Contemporary Poetry
    1. English poetry – 20th century
    I. Wain, John
    821'.9'1408   PR1225

ISBN 0 09 138651 9 non-net
     0 09 138571 7 net

Contents

I wish to thank my wife Eirian for crucial help in preparing this anthology, and its predecessor

Introduction

1

Poetry is a very durable art. All my life I seem to have been listening to people wondering aloud whether it would 'survive', and behold, here I am in middle age and it seems to be surviving better than ever. Not that I am surprised. Poetry, however we define it - and I think the simplest bedrock definition is 'anything that makes language dance and sing as well as just speak' - is evidently a necessity of the human spirit. Every society of which we have record, from ancient Ithaca to modern Australia, has poets. There may be, in a money-centred society, little enough commercial encouragement for them; but a need is a need, and people no more ask how much they will be paid for writing a poem than they ask how much they will be paid for breathing.

Of course poetry changes; change is a condition of life. (The *Oxford Dictionary* defines life as 'state of ceaseless change and functional activity peculiar to organized matter'.) If, for instance, we go back to the early eighteenth century, we find a very clear line of demarcation between popular verse on the one hand and, on the other, what for want of a better term I must call learned or 'polite' poetry - polite not because it avoids indecorous subjects (it doesn't), but because it is cultivated, allusive, presupposing a knowledge of other poetry, having the characteristics of *polis*, the city: written often by learned poets who draw on their learning. The mass of the people have their ballads and songs and rhymed proverbs, their hymns and psalms in church; the cultivated reader has his ode, sonnet and epic. As time goes on there are some comings and goings between these territories; a poem like *Paradise Lost*, re-telling a biblical story at a time when the Bible is in everyone's hands, has a large popular readership; the late medieval ballads, originating in a feudal society, are revived by collectors in the mid-eighteenth century for an audience of bookish people. But, in the main, popular and polite flow contentedly in their clearly marked channels. Only in the twentiety century, when mass communication reaches everyone simultaneously, and a machine-based democracy undermines the old social demarcations, does folk-art lose its popular base and become the preserve of the museums. This in turn affects polite art, which becomes more inbred and, to the average man, more incomprehensible. The broad ground in the middle, where the two might have hoped to meet and achieve a new synthesis, tends to be cluttered with a marketable entertainment-art, a substitute product which is neither genuinely popular in the sense of coming from the people themselves, nor deeply considered enough to appeal to the connoisseur. Here as in other spheres, the merely good is the enemy of the best.

2

It was, I believe, in response to this situation that 'modern' poetry, and the 'modern' arts generally, grew up. I put the word in inverted commas because its use, here, is slightly specialized. The Latin word *modo* means 'just now', and *modernus*, from which we derive our word, is the adjective from it; but of course an attitude characteristic of 'just now' will tend to be forward-looking, impatient of tradition, eager to adapt to change however sweeping, and it is these attitudes that have come to be lumped together as 'modern'. Thus, of two artists working side by side, one might easily be more modern than the other; it might easily be the older who was more modern than the younger.

The modern arts, as they grew up between about 1912 and 1945, were characteristic of an epoch of social impatience. Many people felt that the old social modes, the old political modes, the old personal modes were obsolete. The battle between the young and the old, which is always going on to some extent, was considerably sharpened up in the early years of the century. If we read, say, the novels of the youthful H.G. Wells - *Kipps*, for instance, or *Mr Polly* - we can feel behind them the presence of a new generation knocking on the door. The common people, no longer 'content with their station', liberated from illiteracy by the Education Act of 1870, interested in science and technology, suspicious of the traditional culture that seemed to them a preserve of the better-off, excited by a whiff of Socialist and Fabian ideas as promulgated by William Morris and Shaw – these people were stirring restlessly. The First World War knocked the idealism and optimism out of this impulse to change, but nothing could stop the impulse itself; it became, in the 1920s, more cynical and world-weary without becoming any less dynamic. 'Experiment' was the key-word of the 'twenties, and the artists who made the greatest impact on the young – Picasso, Stravinsky, T. S. Eliot – were those who seemed to promise the most complete break with the past, that past which had produced social injustice, obsolete thinking, and finally the catastrophe of 1914.

The modern artist tended to be cosmopolitan. He tended to assume that there was a minority of forward-looking people, scattered more or less thinly about the globe and mostly in the big cities where publishing, and exhibiting, and the performing arts could most easily be organized. This public, not very numerous anywhere, always a minority, nevertheless formed a large enough body when taken all together, and it was this body to which the modern artist addressed himself. It was partly a matter of life-style. People hung abstract paintings on their walls, went to concerts of atonal music, bought volumes of poetry of whose paraphrasable content they could give no precise account, because it was all part of a demonstration of solidarity with like-minded progressives everywhere, and a protest against dull, conformist, habit-ridden bourgeois life.

All this was perfectly understandable and sympathetic. But as time went on it began to lose some of its magic. These progressive young people married and had children; and the children, by a universal law of nature, were if anything rather bored by the adventurous art that had challenged and stimulated their parents. Modernism in the arts began to seem conventional. Paradoxically, it became a cult of the middle-aged rather than the young. People tend to go through life faithful to the kind of art that aroused their passionate interest in youth; and, as Picasso, Stravinsky and Eliot moved through middle to old age, so did their most devoted adherents.

Naturally this is only part of the picture. A great artist is a great artist, whether or not he is fashionable at this or that moment. Eliot's poems are classics of English literature, and anyone who takes an interest in that literature will read and respond to them. But, though immediate contemporary atti-

11

tudes may not have power to sweep away the great landmarks, they do have power to influence the kind of work that is actually produced. Not only the public, but the artists themselves, showed signs of satiety with the assumptions and procedures of modern art. Their thoughts began to turn towards that long-neglected middle ground. The *avant-garde*, scattered thinly around the world with a small cluster in every capital city, had been well catered for. What of the broader, less specialized public - educated, interested, seeking to have their lives enriched by the arts, but not primarily concerned with experiment and not necessarily equating art with social change - who existed everywhere?

And, once again, social patterns were reflected in the arts. Where the generation who made a star of H. G. Wells had been produced by ground-floor universal education, so in the years since the Second World War there has been a new public produced by the expansion of the universities. Higher education is no longer the preserve of a small, privileged *élite*. It has become, in Europe as in America, a normal expectation of intelligent people. Naturally this has led to arguments as to whether its standards have, or have not, slipped. But one thing is clear. Since 1950 there has grown up, all over the western world and doubtless not only there, a public large enough to be an effective audience for the artist, informed and thoughtful enough not to be satisfied with the machine-products turned out by television and the popular press, and yet not thinking of itself in minority terms as an *avant-garde* committed to leaving everyone else out of sight.

Not that this new public is conservative-minded. In many of the arts - in theatre, for instance - it has shown itself hospitable to attempts to break out of old moulds. (It costs so much money to put on a play that theatre managements are especially cautious and resistant to change: an empty theatre can bankrupt a lot of people, so that it is the little shoe-string companies, putting on their productions in the upper rooms of pubs or even in the street, that have been able to show most initiative.) But there was, in the previous generation, a conservatism that underlay modernism itself, a feeling that unless an artist was experimental and difficult to understand, he couldn't be serious. And this has now, demonstrably, gone.

That withdrawal from the purer forms of modernism, that emergence of a public not primarily concerned with seeing itself as an *avant-garde*, provides us with one avenue of approach to the poetry of the last thirty years. Another is the fact, perhaps explicable and perhaps not, that there has been in those years no single commanding figure or knot of figures. This, by itself, is the largest single difference between the state of poetry before 1945 and since. Twentieth-century poetry had been dominated for so long by the achievements of a few men of genius: Yeats, already acknowledged as an important poet before 1900, was not in fashion throughout his long life, but *The Tower* (1928), perhaps the finest single volume of poems published this century, brought him back to mid-stage, and his magnificent *Last Poems* appeared in 1940, the year after he died, so that he was a conspicuous presence to the end. Eliot had become the idol of the young with *The Waste Land* in 1922; twenty years later he was publishing, one at a time, the *Four Quartets*, and during the whole of that period he had been the acknowledged leader of the modernist wing of English poetry, with the pioneer figure of Ezra Pound, to whom Eliot consistently acknowledged a crucial debt, clearly visible in the background. After W. H. Auden exploded on to the scene with *Poems* (1930), he became a hero to the younger generation of poets and readers, but Eliot was still the powerful uncle-figure. Dylan Thomas began publishing in 1934 and in the next ten years added his name to the short list of poets with a wide following and a deep influence. Other poets, sometimes of the highest quality, grouped themselves or were grouped in relation to these giants.

That was, in essentials, the situation in 1945. Since then, much fine work has been produced (I hope this anthology will, at the very least, put *that* fact beyond doubt) but there has been no individual poet as commanding, as closely followed by a devoted and even fanatical band of followers, as Eliot or Auden or Thomas. (Yeats, the most over-arching presence of all, did not have 'followers' in this sense. His path was too lonely, his art, like Shakespeare's, too large-scale to be reproduced by imitation.) Of course people have favourites among the more recent poets. Philip Larkin is mine, very closely followed by Tony Connor; Ted Hughes has admirers who think him the finest living poet, and so do Geoffrey Hill and, increasingly, Seamus Heaney – to go no further into the invidious business of picking out individual names. But that's the point — it *is* invidious. There are so many poets of strength and individuality, so many offerings of genuine worth, that to name A without naming B and C comes to seem an insult, and if B and C then certainly D, E, F and on down to Z.

3

One of the things one notices when reading contemporary poetry in bulk, as I have been doing for the purposes of this book, is the wide variety of ways in which poets approach the question of form. In some epochs of literary history, poets are on the whole content with the forms which have been working well for their civilization, expressing its thoughts and aspirations and dreams, telling its stories, portraying its scenes: thus the Augustan poets, more or less from 1660 to 1750, were largely content with the end-stopped couplet (called the 'heroic' couplet because it was associated with epic poetry, as in Dryden's famous translation of Virgil and Pope's even more famous two translations of Homer), or with certain well-tried lyric measures; again, the Victorians, willing though they were to experiment with a wide range of forms, tended to feel happier with patterns that had been used before and were associated with recognizable purposes: ten-syllable blank verse for high narrative, the sonnet for passionate reverie or formal address, the ode (however structured) for lofty rhetoric and high meditation. When the modern idiom came in, the reigning conventions were at once passed under searching and sceptical review: to express a modern view of the world, it seemed to many, must involve breaking the old forms. But what to replace them with? Only the weaker brethren, the very minor talents, imagined that the answer could be, 'with nothing'.

'Free' verse, at one time generally called *vers libre* because it was thought to be an import from France, has of course been used widely by modern poets in every country. (In modern Arabic literature, for instance, where the traditional procedures seem too bound up with a wholesale retention of the orthodox Muslim past and an acceptance of its rigid social patterns, it is virtually universal.) But, from the beginning, poets of any quality have realized that it is not enough simply to write prose and arrange it typographically as verse; they have acknowledged the truth of T. S. Eliot's blunt warning, 'No *vers* is *libre* for the man who wants to do a good job.' And, only a little further back from that position, there is the attitude expressed by another great American poet, Robert Frost, when he said, 'Writing poetry without metre is like playing tennis without a net.' The comparison is not frivolous. A game, once the rules have been accepted by both sides, can be a contest in which real qualities are involved - skill, judgement, courage, endurance; if it is merely random movement, nothing is involved. Similarly in art. The conventions - and the word 'convention' means 'a coming together', an agreement about a basic diagram of action - provide the framework against which the raw emotion of the poem can define itself - or, if you will, beat itself like an animal against the bars of the cage. 'He tames his love,' said Donne, 'fetters it in verse,' and the harsh metaphor from imprisonment brings home the basic fact that art is one of the ways in which the human being tries to deal with realities that might otherwise become unmanageable. We might put it more gently by saying that form, in any art, makes a frame for the picture, a vessel into which the imperishable fluid can be poured so that it does not merely run away into the sand.

A look through this book will indicate the poets' continuing concern for form and how it can help them. Take, for instance, D. M. Thomas's *sestina*, 'The journey'. Since it concerns a painful, repetitive situation - visiting a mother who is old and ailing, and whose world is so far apart from her son's that he feels his visits to her resemble pilgrimages to natural phenomena like moors and lakes that have no language, that one goes to just because they are *there* - it needs a form that suggests coming back, again and again, to certain inescapable bedrock facts. The *sestina* requires six stanzas of six lines; the stanzas do not rhyme, but the words that come at the end of a line, once laid down in the opening stanza, are then used (in any order)* in the other five. Finally, as if to tie the whole parcel

*In English, that is. As originally used in Provençal, the chime-words had to occur in a prescribed order. But our ways are more lenient.

15

with a knot, come three lines in which all six chime-words are used, either at the end of a line or at mid-point. The choice of this form for such a poem as 'The journey' is very apt. It is, of course, an ironic use of the form: the original invention of the *sestina* is generally credited to Arnaut Daniel, the vivid late-twelfth-century Provençal poet so much admired by Dante, and in its first phase it was a favourite with Provençal poets who wrote in the springtime of European civilization, and expressed their feelings directly and lyrically. Only much later – in our time, indeed – did the form reveal its possibilities for such statements as D. M. Thomas makes here: wearier, more qualified, with a tenderness always struggling to get out from under the layers of *ennui* and a sense of duty. But feelings like this are real too, as characteristic of our age as the more open ardours of the troubadours were of theirs, and the typical modern *sestina* is a tribute to the continued vitality and usefulness of Arnaut Daniel's form.

That is what I had in mind when describing D. M. Thomas's use of the *sestina* form as 'ironic' – giving it a twist, bringing out qualities in it that were not envisaged among its original purposes and may even seem to run counter to these purposes. And in fact many contemporary poets use traditional forms in a way that brings out new qualities in them. Consider the rhymed stanzas in Peter Levi's 'For poets in prison without trial'. Fundamentally, this is the four-line stanza with a ten-syllable line, traditional in English poetry – the stanza of Dryden's 'Annus mirabilis' or Gray's 'Elegy in a country churchyard'. But Levi has given it a new music by loosening the rhythm and displacing the rhymes a little. In a society like that of Dryden or Gray, when people dressed in ornate and stately clothes and a formal dignity was part of daily life, the firm, measured tread and precise rhymes of their poetry were a fitting reflection of qualities they prized and might reasonably aim at. The same forms will do duty today, bringing with them a reassuring sense of continuity, of a living link with those who went before, but to make them do this duty involves adapting them to the more casual, off-hand, informal patterns of modern life. Thus, to come back to Peter Levi, we find that his characteristic rhythm is the English ten-syllable line with the iambic feet reversed here and there, making them heavy-light instead of light-heavy: so that where Gray, for instance, wrote

And leaves the world to darkness and to me

Levi will write

thinking how mother earth keeps us at it

or

Bigger breasted than birds, it is breathing.

Rhyme itself brings out some interesting attitudes. Over the centuries, many poets have found it a help. Not that it is essential to poetry; neither the ancient Greeks nor the Romans used it; European poetry knows nothing of rhyme till the middle ages. As Milton remarked disdainfully, it was 'the invention of a barbarous age' - though he showed himself able to use that barbarous invention brilliantly when it suited his purpose. That, of course, is the point: rhyme often does suit the purposes of poetry. Imagine a comic lyric or a popular song without it! But its uses can be stately as well as light; it can make a lyric haunting, or the encapsulation of a thought unforgettable; it can impart urgency:

Sink me the ship, master gunner! Sink her, split her in twain!
Sooner into the hands of God than into the hands of Spain!

In this book, the gleefully skipping rhymes of Ted Hughes's 'Music on the moon' or the complex rhyme-scheme, forming a creative tension with the conversational diction, of Clive James's 'Letter from Leningrad' will get us started. Very few of these poems have been chosen on formal grounds, yet the collection, now that it is put together, turns out to contain just about every kind of rhyme and non-rhyme. Some poets never use rhyme at all; others, like John Betjeman, seem never to write without it. Some poets use traditional rhyme-schemes; others, like Dylan Thomas, invent their own. Others again allow rhyme to come and go within the same poem. Obviously it is no accident when John Heath-Stubbs's beautifully dreamy 'River song', having avoided rhyme all the way through, suddenly uses it in the second and fourth lines of the final stanza; it brings the poem, musically, to a close. Or a lightly-rhyming pattern will hold the stanzas in place, prevent the poem from wobbling; in C. Day Lewis's 'Walking away',

17

rhymes bind together the first, third and fifth lines of each stanza.

Again, rhymes can be exact, giving a finality of statement, as in Marvell's

> ... always at my back I hear
> Time's winged chariot hurrying near

or they can be softly chiming, deliberately near-missing, to suggest meditation and subtlety. Philip Larkin in 'Going, going' or John Ormond in 'Definition of a waterfall' use strict rhymes; Anne Stevenson's 'Resurrection' uses the soft hazy echo. In each case the poem dictates its own needs, and the first thing the poet has to do is listen. Auden's 'The shield of Achilles' demands tight formal rhymes; Tony Connor in 'Approaching Bolton' moves the rhymes slightly apart to give a gentle, musing effect.

As with rhyme, so with stanza form. Not for nothing have poets traditionally used the stanza; the word itself reminds us of our debt to Italy, where the word means a resting-place, somewhere to stand; reading a poem in stanzas is like walking through a succession of beautiful rooms rather than trudging down a long straight corridor. Very often, stanza form by itself can do the work of rhyme, giving the same singing and chiming effect without actual rhyme-words. Tennyson's 'Tears, idle tears', for instance, has no rhymes, yet many people who know it well are unaware of the fact; the four-line stanzas are of a kind that usually rhyme, and they are very musical, so we read it like a rhymed poem. In the same way a great many of the poems in this book are arranged in stanza form; the eye takes them in like that because of their arrangement on the page, and as a result we *hear* them in stanzas, whether we read them aloud or hear them inside our head, though they dispense with the rhymes that traditionally staked out the stanza. Examples would be John Ormond's 'The cathedral builders' or D. M. Thomas's 'Stone'.

So, in reading this book, keep an eye out for the formal aspects of the poems. To pay attention to these things is not a fussy pedantry. On the contrary, it is essential, if we are to appreciate anything, from a grand piano to a space-ship, to have an appreciative eye for the processes that have gone into its making. A poem's form is part of its system of signals. When Auden, for instance, writes a wry, humorous, pitying account of finding himself compelled to set mouse-traps, he writes it in the hexameters of classical Latin poetry: and this is part of the poem's atmosphere and therefore of its meaning: the metre of the *Aeneid* used to talk about mice! The touching absurdity of life! - After all, to the mice themselves this is a life and death matter, as serious as anything described in Homer or Virgil.

4

The reader who wants to get the best out of this book will begin by noting that, though self-sufficient, it takes off from a selection I made in 1961, and also published by Hutchinson, under the title *Anthology of Modern Poetry*. The object of that book was to give some account, in introduction and selection, of the classical phase of modern poetry, from the founding fathers - as far back as Hopkins in the 1870s - to the inheritors of the tradition in the 1940s and 1950s. For that reason, it included both English and American poets, because the story it had to tell would otherwise have been incomplete. And it described a movement that had a coherent historical shape: a clearly marked beginning, a zenith, and . . .

And what? An end? I am not sure, and it will, I think, be a long time before anyone can be sure. Whether 'modern' poetry, the poetry based on the techniques and attitudes that were known as 'modern' between 1912 and 1950, has a future in England I simply do not know. It may quite easily have one future in England and another in America; it very demonstrably has followed, and will follow, a different course outside the English-speaking world: in southern Europe, say, or Latin America. But, as I started out by saying, the word 'modern' never had a purely temporal significance. It referred to a spirit, an attitude, a set of assumptions. And one of the things that has happened since 1945 is that this spirit, these assumptions, have been modified here, weakened there, assimilated to the point of disappearance in some areas, quietly forgotten in others. Contemporary poetry, as we have known it for twenty years and will continue to know it till the next big upheaval, need not necessarily be 'modern'.

The classical phase of modern poetry still retains its importance. It is full of fine things. In breadth and range of vision, 'modern' poetry has already taken its place beside the poetry of the romantic epoch, of the Augustan age or the renaissance. It is, like them, a period, which readers of poetry will always study; with interest, with excitement, with admiration; with a profound sense of gratitude to the artists who have drawn back a curtain on the world and helped us to see and know it. But, though we study those great periods, we do not feel ourselves to be living in them. (Except, of course, by virtue of that imaginative identification without which nothing human can be studied at all.) We look at them as adventures of the human spirit which can incite and strengthen us for our own adventure, rather than as direct reaction to the world we have to inhabit in our days.

Since 1945, it has become increasingly clear that a similar process has overtaken the classical phase of 'modern' poetry, and perhaps of 'modern' art generally. Hence the need for another book, taking the story from the end of the Second World War up to now.

Hence, also, the fact that this present volume, unlike its predecessor, does not contain any work by American poets. During the classic phase of modern poetry, the English and American stems were inter-twined; the whole modern movement, in the English language, was given its initial thrust by two expatriate Americans, Eliot and Pound, themselves working largely from French models. But, as the years have gone by, English and American poetry have settled down into their respective channels. There have been, indeed – notably among the 'protest' poets of the 1960s – English poets who have worked to American blueprints; but their work seems to me to belong to a sub-category of American poetry rather than to our own tradition. American poetry since the war has been full of energy and interest; but it is not represented here for the same reason that French or Italian or Hungarian poetry are not represented: it is very fine, but it happens to be something else.

Oddments, inklings, omens, moments

Oddments, as when
you see through skin,
when flowers appear
to be eavesdropping,
or music somewhere
declares your mood;
when sleep fulfils
a feel of dying
or fear makes ghosts
of clothes on a chair.

Inklings, as when
some room rhymes
with a lost time,
or a book reads
like a well-known dream;
when a smell recalls
portraits, funerals,
when a wish happens
or a mirror sees
through distances.

Omens, as when
a shadow from nowhere
falls on a wall,
when a bird seems
to mimic your name,
when a cat eyes you
as though it knew
or, heavy with augury,
a crow caws
cras cras from a tree.

continued

Moments, as when
the air's awareness
makes guesses true,
when a hand's touch
speaks past speech
or when, in poise,
two sympathies
lighten each other,
and love occurs
like song, like weather.

Alastair Reid

Prose poem towards a definition of itself

When in public poetry should take off its clothes and wave
to the nearest person in sight; It should be seen in the
company of thieves and lovers rather than that of journalists
and publishers. On sighting mathematicians it should
unhook the algebra from their minds and replace it with
poetry; on sighting poets it should unhook poetry from the
minds and replace it with algebra: it should touch those
people who despise being touched, it should fall in love with
children and woo them with fairytales; it should wait on the
landing for two years for its mates to come home then go
outside and find them all dead.

When the electricity fails it should wear dark glasses and pretend to be blind. It should guide those who are safe into the middle of busy roads and leave them there. It should scatter woodworm into the bedrooms of all peglegged men, not being afraid to hurt the innocent; it should shout Evil! Evil! Evil! from the roofs of stock exchanges. It should not pretend to be a clerk or a librarian. It is the eventual sameness of contradictions. It should never weep unless it is alone, and then only after it has covered the mirrors and sealed up the cracks.

Poetry should seek out pale and lyrical couples and wander with them into stables, neglected bedrooms, engineless cars, unsafe forests, for A Final Good Time. It should enter burning factories too late to save anybody. It should pay no attention to its name.

Poetry should be seen lying by the side of road accidents, hissing from unlit gas-rings. It should scrawl the nymph's secret on her teacher's blackboard, offer her a worm saying: Inside this is a tiny apple. At dawn it should leave the bedroom and catch the first bus home to its wife. At dusk it should chat up a girl nobody wants. It should be seen standing on the ledge of a skyscraper, on a bridge with a brick tied around its heart. Poetry is the monster hiding in a child's dark room, it is the scar on a beautiful person's face. It is the last blade of grass being picked from the city park.

Brian Patten

Visitations VI

The gull hundreds of miles below him -
  Was it the Muse?
The cloud thousands of miles above him -
  Was it the Muse?
The river intoning his saga over and over,
The siren blaring her long farewell to Dover,
The grasshopper snipping scissors in the clover -
  Were they the Muse or no?

So those who carry this birthright and this burden
Regardless of all else must always listen
On the odd chance some fact or freak or phantom
Might tell them what they want, might burst the cordon
Which isolates them from their inmost vision.

The cradle thousands of years behind him -
  Was it the Muse?
The coffin a headstone's throw before him -
  Is it the Muse?
The clock that is ever impeding, ever abetting,
The bed that is ever remembering, ever forgetting,
The sun ever rising and setting, unrising, unsetting -
  Are they the Muse or no?

So those endowed with such a doom and heirloom
When others can be carefree must be careful
(Though sometimes, when the rest are careful, carefree),
Must wait for the unimmediately apparent
And grasp the Immediate - fairly or unfairly.

The world one millimetre beyond him -
  Is it the Muse?
The soul untold light years inside him -
  Is it the Muse?
The python of the past with coils unending,
The lion of the present roaring, rending,
The grey dove of the future still descending -
  Are they the Muse? Or no?

Louis MacNeice

The tractor in spring

Driving the solid field about sunset,
under a wood half picked out in colour,
I fume coarsely along in the fine air,
thinking how mother earth keeps us at it,
swathed in her withering rose and violet,
her thin liquids, her cold and lasting fire.

Everywhere the same lines show,
tree, cloud, furrow and sky overhead
rounded with seed, leaden as an eyelid,
and everything they promise will come true,
a sky so blue it makes rock look blue,
a wood so green it hides the glittering seed.

The earth knows how to breed and to feed us,
her raw juices are still running at least,
the tractor mumbling at its throatiest
speaks to earth in a kind of lover's voice.
All day like larks we rattle around loose
but twilight finds us fumbling with the breast.

Maker and speaker and machine,
and everything said, everything done
gurgles its gritty pap at this season.
More birds make music than can be seen,
dissolving their sweet names in acid green.
The same heat works on everyone.

I want words whose existence is this,
the rough soil and the root work in them,
praising heaven I ever took for theme
this planet, its unnatural wishes,
common reason and human justice,
and growth of life, the last increase of time.

Peter Levi

Digging

Between my finger and my thumb
The squat pen rests; snug as a gun.

Under my window, a clean rasping sound
When the spade sinks into gravelly ground:
My father, digging. I look down

Till his straining rump among the flowerbeds
Bends low, comes up twenty years away
Stooping in rhythm through potato drills
Where he was digging.

The coarse boot nestled on the lug, the shaft
Against the inside knee was levered firmly.
He rooted out tall tops, buried the bright edge deep
To scatter new potatoes that we picked
Loving their cool hardness in our hands.

By God, the old man could handle a spade.
Just like his old man.

My grandfather cut more turf in a day
Than any other man on Toner's bog.
Once I carried him milk in a bottle
Corked sloppily with paper. He straightened up
To drink it, then fell to right away
Nicking and slicing neatly, heaving sods
Over his shoulder, going down and down
For the good turf. Digging.

The cold smell of potato mould, the squelch and slap
Of soggy peat, the curt cuts of an edge
Through living roots awaken in my head.
But I've no spade to follow men like them.

Between my finger and my thumb
The squat pen rests.
I'll dig with it.

Seamus Heaney

Stone

The first book of a poet should be called *Stone*
Or *Evening*, expressing in a single word
The modesty of being part of the earth,
The goodness of evening and stone, beyond the poet.

The second book should have a name blushing
With a great generality, such as *My Sister Life*,
Shocking in its pride, even more in its modesty:
Exasperated, warm, teasing, observant, tender.

Later books should withdraw into a mysterious
Privacy such as we all make for ourselves:
The White Stag or *Plantain*. Or include the name
Of the place at which his book falls open.

There is also the seventh book, perhaps, the seventh,
And called *The Seventh Book* because it is not published,
The one that a child thinks he could have written,
Made of the firmest stone and clearest leaves,

That a people keep alive by, keep alive.

D. M. Thomas

On the cliff

Between the scented soap works
and cloud-capped cooling towers,
I walked one summer evening
swishing the soot-stained flowers.

Below, the black river
snaked around the racecourse,
drudging to distant sea
the dregs of commerce,

and huge across my vision
under the streaky sky
from Chapel Reach to Pomona Dock
the changing city lay,

swarming invisibly
with its intricate, restless hordes
of common humanity -
the keepers of the Word.

All I have accepted
to exercise heart and wit:
the unpredictable home
of the ever-unlikely poet.

There on the shifting cliff
where nothing built will stand -
local eruption of a fault
that runs across England -

I watched the lights come on,
and listened to a lover
coaxing a silent girl
under near cover,

and farther off the yells
of children at some chase;
voices much like my own -
the accent of the place.

The accent of the place!
My claim to a shared load
of general circumstance
with the hidden multitude.

Yet strange despite the wish,
because my chosen task
was the making of poems,
I shivered in the dusk,

aware that my shining city
did not care one jot
for me as its celebrant,
or whether I wrote or not.

I might have been unborn,
or else long dead,
but before I reached my home
I had perfected

the sociable, lonely poet,
a rueful one-man sect,
in an ignorant, ugly city -
his God-given subject.

Tony Connor

Cathedral builders

They climbed on sketchy ladders towards God,
With winch and pulley hoisted hewn rock into heaven,
Inhabited sky with hammers, defied gravity,
Deified stone, took up God's house to meet Him,

And came down to their suppers and small beer;
Every night slept, lay with their smelly wives,
Quarrelled and cuffed the children, lied,
Spat, sang, were happy or unhappy,

And every day took to the ladders again;
Impeded the rights of way of another summer's
Swallows, grew greyer, shakier, became less inclined
To fix a neighbour's roof of a fine evening,

Saw naves sprout arches, clerestories soar,
Cursed the loud fancy glaziers for their luck,
Somehow escaped the plague, got rheumatism,
Decided it was time to give it up,

To leave the spire to others; stood in the crowd
Well back from the vestments at the consecration,
Envied the fat bishop his warm boots,
Cocked up a squint eye and said, 'I bloody did that.'

John Ormond

Song of the death-watch beetle

Here come I, the death-watch beetle
Chewing away at the great cathedral;

Gnawing the mediaeval beams
And the magnificent carved rood screen

Gorging on gospels and epistles
From the illuminated missals;

As once I ate the odes of Sappho
And the histories of Manetho,

The lost plays of Euripides
And all the thought of Parmenides.

The Sibyl's leaves which the wind scattered,
And great aunt Delia's love letters.

Turn down the lamp in the cooling room:
There stand I with my little drum.

Death. Watch. You are watching death.
Blow out the lamp with your last breath.

John Heath-Stubbs

Rembrandt's late self-portraits

You are confronted with yourself. Each year
The pouches fill, the skin is uglier.
You give it all unflinchingly. You stare
Into yourself, beyond. Your brush's care
Runs with self-knowledge. Here

Is a humility at one with craft.
There is no arrogance. Pride is apart
From this self-scrutiny. You make light drift
The way you want. Your face is bruised and hurt
But there is still love left.

Love of the art and others. To the last
Experiment went on. You stared beyond
Your age, the times. You also plucked the past
And tempered it. Self-portraits understand,
And old age can divest,

With truthful changes, us of fear of death.
Look, a new anguish. There, the bloated nose,
The sadness and the joy. To paint's to breathe,
And all the darknesses are dared. You chose
What each must reckon with.

Elizabeth Jennings

Words made of water

Men meet and part;
But meeting men today
I find them frightened,
Frightened and insolent,
Distrustful as myself.
We turn arrogantly toward one another,
Caged in dogmatical dazzle.
Our eyes shine like thin torchlight.
Conflicting truths, we dazzle one another.
Never lately have I known men meet
With only darkness, quite anonymous,
Perched up between them on a song no bird
Would answer for in sunlight.
I have watched carefully but never once
Have I seen the little heaps,
The co-ordinated fragments of muscle, brain, bone,
Creep steadfastly as ants across the planet,
Quite lost in their own excess of contraries,
Make signals, ask for answers,
Humbly and heavily from those they know
Are equally ignorant.

Looking about the streets I find the answers,
Thin blobs of light, enamelled price-lists, brawling,
An impatient competition
Between all those who all know all the answers.

I find also certain bits of paper,
Matchsticks, sodden or cracked or still with safety heads,
Cigarette douts and their empty packets,
And also water,
Water that is stagnant
Or water flowing slowly down the gutter.

continued

I sometimes think that dead men live in water,
That their ghosts inhabit the stagnant puddles,
Their barges float with the gutter water,
That they are waiting patiently as water
Until the world is redeemed by doubt,
By each man's love for all those different answers
Dead men have dropped on sundry bits of paper,
From glances blue as smoke, now quite extinguished.

My womenfolk find these thoughts troubling.
Action becomes impossible: choice is impossible
To those who think such things.
On thoughts like these no man ever grew fat.

J. Burns Singer

1973

Lean, mean year, breeder of obituaries.
Funereal year, you earned a black border.
Half-masted year, we thankfully cover you over.

You claimed the long-lived ones, Casals, Picasso;
Neruda and Chile both, in one rank breath.
You gorged yourself on armies, tribes, and children.

Robbing the present to enrich the past,
you leave us as a string of cruel ciphers.
Your notes and dates are permanent in stone.

Corrosive months, counting us down in deathbells.
Gray ghoulish months of crows and cruel weather.
Meat-eating months, you trained us in despair.

Although we spite you now by seeing you out,
be confident that you will be remembered,
bitch year, burier, bearer of famous dark.

Alastair Reid

Verses for the 60th birthday
of Thomas Stearns Eliot

1

By that evening window where
His accurate eye keeps Woburn Square
Under perpetual judgement so
That only the happy can come and go
About these gardens and not be
Tested in that dark neutrality,
Which, in between love and disgust,
Hates most of all its own mistrust,
I see this gentle and gothic man
Tame Apollyon with a pen.

continued

2

I never know the juggernauts
Go bulldozing through my thoughts
So that everything I own
Is trod down and overthrown
Without remembering that worse
Than thunder in the hearse
Is the supernatural sigh
Of illusions as they die -
But in the room of Eliot
The visions whistle as they rot.

3

To him the dead twig in the gutter
Cries across all law to utter
Confidences that would bring
Tears to the eyes of anything.
But that set imperial face
Has looked down on our disgrace
And, without betraying so
Little as a twinge of sorrow,
Seen all grief begin again -
A gentle and long-suffering man.

4

Outside the huge negations pass
Like whirlwinds writing on the grass
Inscriptions teaching us that all
The lessons are ephemeral;
But as the huge negations ride
And depredate all things outside
His window, he puts out his hand
And writes with whirlwinds on the ground
Asseverations that tame
The great negations with his name.

George Barker

New Year's Eve poem 1965

When Eliot died it made him seem human,
nineteen sixty five has been
one hoarse tap tap tap of a black stick,
black water dripping on a dead train.

I never had a dream so powerful
as when Eliot died. He pulled this year
like a black car over a dead moor
in a blue mist, through words and things of fear.

When he died I went into real mourning,
poems are wrecked, this is the sea-bottom:
the anchor-chains of reason drag and swing
backwards and forwards with a squeak like doom.

Now say seven hundred years ago
Dante died: heavenly innocence
like a wild bush of roses cannot grow,
and the starving forest has broken its fence.

Since his time nature is ingrowing;
thinking of Dante what I wonder most
is when the inferno like a complete dream
will eat my poems and swallow my ghost.

No one has spoken as clearly as they did
or in such austere words of poetry:
the angel of language is visible,
the fire stands in the air over the tree.

Heaven is intellectual, to feel
at home there goes beyond man and woman:
and I have never dreamed of such a thing.
When Eliot died, it made him seem human.

Peter Levi

Elegy for W. H. Auden

Stones endure as your first and last things.
The carpet slippers, the leather skin,
The incorrigible laughter inaccurately aped,

Those late epigrams which obviously were
The acute desperation of that laughter –
These are forgotten almost already.

But the stone your student hand held gently,
Schoolboy hair flopped over years later,
The limestone which reminded you of love

And caught the last strains of your lyrical perceptions,
The walks out of Italy into Austria,
All that grey North which you set glowing –

Yes, it is geology, quarries and tools,
The precise tap on the finished fossil,
And last the shuffle on Christ Church cobbles,

The cobbles you must have stared at rather
Than look up as Wren's Tom trembled your hours –
All these are a life you refused to surrender.

No glass-cases and no museums.
All your grand operas opened into caves
Where your Orators shout and your Mirror is shining.

The Sea stands still but your landscape moves.

Elizabeth Jennings

Merlin

I will consider the outnumbering dead:
For they are the husks of what was rich seed.
Now, should they come together to be fed,
They would outstrip the locusts' covering tide.

Arthur, Elaine, Mordred; they are all gone
Among the raftered galleries of bone.
By the long barrows of Logres they are made one,
And over their city stands the pinnacled corn.

Geoffrey Hill

Druid's circle

The few squat leaning rocks in a loose ring
are a disappointment to all that climb
the mountain track to see them. They are nothing
like Auschwitz, Belsen, or Buchenwald. No crime

against humanity lingers in the air
of this place. The so-called 'Sacrificial
Stone' is a boring flat expanse, bare
of any hint of blood. It doesn't look especial

in the least—except for the roughly scratched
initials: a confused palimpsest
of clumsy letters cross-hatched
on its surface. To most people the trip's a waste

of time, and, if the women shudder,
the men light pipes, the children fret,
it is the wild-eyed ba-ba and scatter
of all that moving mutton, the sight

continued

of so much horizon, and the air,
appalling in its emptiness,
that makes them loath to explore further,
and sends them townwards, laughing with distress.

Tony Connor

The Tollund man

1

Some day I will go to Aarhus
To see his peat-brown head,
The mild pods of his eye-lids,
His pointed skin cap.

In the flat country nearby
Where they dug him out,
His last gruel of winter seeds
Caked in his stomach,

Naked except for
The cap, noose and girdle,
I will stand a long time.
Bridegroom to the goddess,

She tightened her torc on him
And opened her fen,
Those dark juices working
Him to a saint's kept body,

Trove of the turfcutters'
Honeycombed workings.
Now his stained face
Reposes at Aarhus.

40

2

I could risk blasphemy,
Consecrate the cauldron bog
Our holy ground and pray
Him to make germinate

The scattered, ambushed
Flesh of labourers,
Stockinged corpses
Laid out in the farmyards,

Tell-tale skin and teeth
Flecking the sleepers
Of four young brothers, trailed
For miles along the lines.

3

Something of his sad freedom
As he rode the tumbril
Should come to me, driving,
Saying the names

Tollund, Grabaulle, Nebelgard,
Watching the pointing hands
Of country people,
Not knowing their tongue.

Out there in Jutland
In the old man-killing parishes
I will feel lost,
Unhappy and at home.

Seamus Heaney

Sleep now

In memory of Wilfred Owen

Sleep now,
Your blood moving in the quiet wind;
No longer afraid of the rabbits
Hurrying through the tall grass
Or the faces laughing from
The beach and among cold trees.

Sleep now,
Alone in the sleeves of grief,
Listening to clothes falling
And your flesh touching God;
To the chatter and backslapping
Of Christ meeting heroes of war.

Sleep now,
Your words have passed
The lights shining from the East
And the sound of flack
Raping graves and emptying seasons.

You do not hear the dry wind pray
Or the children play a game called soldiers
In the street.

Brian Patten

Lorca

Lorca
walking
in a red-light
district at night
heard one of his own songs
being sung
by a whore

he was moved
as if the stars
and the lanterns
changed places

neither the song
to himself
belonged
nor the girl
to her humiliation
nothing
belonged to anyone

when she stopped singing
it went on

death must be a poor thing
a poor thing

D.M. Thomas

For poets in prison without trial

All day teaching in some classroom
I can hear your maddened pens,
scratch, scratch, where human foreknowledge comes home,
O images of violence,

continued

O condemned poets, O dead who write
with iron pens in your unresonant cells,
and into mere blackness of the wasting night
drift out like solemn cries of ruined walls,

O dying poets in your terrible rooms,
breathe out your useless messages, your fact
to the inconsequential gaoler when he comes,
the inevitable beauty, passionate and abstract,

and O if some confusion of daylight
drops in the end like leaves on your faces,
then make your eyes star-purple, planet-bright,
like natural forces, echoless voices.

Peter Levi

The commuted sentence

Shut me not alive away
From the light of every day
Hang me rather by the neck to die
Against a morning sky.

Oh shut me not behind a prison wall
I have a horror of this sort of place
Where I may sit and count the hours pass
And never see a smiling human face.

Here is all straight and narrow as a tomb
Oh shut me not within a little room.

Stevie Smith

from *Wildtrack*

Khasan Israelov, dead in an unknown grave,
I speak in a voice that wishes it were yours.

The Chechen-Ingush, a mountain people in the northern Caucasus,
resisted domination by Catherine the Great of Russia, and were
not finally subdued till 1859; they revolted against the Czars in
1867, 1877 and 1905, and after the Soviets came to power they
continued to resist absorption and collectivization. They rebelled in
1930, and were crushed. In 1941, the Chechen-Ingush struck for
their freedom one last time, under the leadership of a young poet,
Khasan Israelov. Stalin's answer was to obliterate the entire
nation by execution and mass deportation on February 23, 1944.
Under the direction of General Serov, the entire operation,
whereby 500,000 people were swept off to death or slavery, took
just twenty-four hours.

1

All those who knew you are dispersed or dead
five hundred thousand people wiped away
corpses or prisoners to the last one.
But listen, Khasan Israelov, where you lie.
I speak in a voice that wishes it were yours.
Listen, Khasan, with your mud-stopped ear.

2

I saw your mountains once, not far away.
In the cold Caucasus I saw them lie
as the eagle sees them, high-shining, one by one.
They know you, Khasan, still, though you are dead.
The wind whose tunes put magic in your ear
whirls in the crannies where the wild goats lie.

continued

3

Eryri or Wicklow, half a world away
I tread on hill-paths that were never yours
and pluck the fragrant heather where I lie.
Mountains are many, but their voice is one,
still crying freedom! into the world's ear,
though by each bluff stiffen the defiant dead.

4

Climb with me, Khasan, till bitterness is dead.
I have not the strength to face an end like yours.
But take this homage, do not turn away.
I hear your mountain music, though my ear
is dulled with cowardice: you are the one
to guide me where the quiet heroes lie.

5

Khasan, your written chronicle is a brief one.
Such sagas are banned from the captive ear.
Soldiers have killed, now bureaucrats must lie.
Five hundred thousand truths to sponge away.
If your name lives, the victory will be yours.
Your strength cannot be tamed now you are dead.

6

The wild chamois is your symbol, if you need one:
Who, chased to the final edge where the hunt stops dead,
Leaps down, with a delicate madness much like yours.
May its gentle ghost be welcome where your bones lie,
Who thought rather to throw life steeply away
Than make a story pleasant to the huntsman's ear!

Khasan, only courage like yours can burn hatred away.
Unstop your ear: pity me from where you lie:
Climb with me, turbulent one, till bitterness is dead!

John Wain

No more Mozart

High to the right a hill of trees,
a fuselage of branches,
reflects German moonlight
like dull armour.
Sieg heil!

Higher still, one moon migrates deathwards,
a white temper between clouds.
To the left, the other slides
undulating on the black
oiled, rippling reservoir.

Can't sleep for Mozart,
and on the winter glass
a shilling's worth of glitter.

The German streets tonight
are soaped in moonlight.
The streets of Germany are clean
like the hands of Lady Macbeth.

Back in bed the eyes close, do not sleep.
Achtung! Achtung!
Someone is breathing nearby,
someone not accounted for.

Now, of course, no more Mozart.
With eyes closed still
the body touches itself, takes stock.
Above the hands the thin wrists
attached to them; and on the wrists
the lampshade material.
Also the little hairs that can be pulled.

continued

The eyes open:
the German earth is made of helmets;
the wind seeps through a deep
frost hole that is somewhere else
carrying the far Jew-sounds of railway trucks.

Nothing is annulled:
the blood vow, the undecorated cry,
someone robbed of his name,
Then silence again.

Afterwards:
the needle rests on a record
with nothing on that record turning,
neither sound nor silence,
for it is sleep at last.

There, the fugitive body has arrived
at the stink of nothing.
And twelve million eyes
in six million heads
stare in the same direction.

Outside, the electrician works
inside his cloud, silently,
and the reservoir darkens.

Germany 1970   *Dannie Abse*

48

A letter from Leningrad
To Michael Frayn

1

Dear *Michael*, here in *Leningrad*
The wind unseasonably chill
For *April* ought to make me sad,
And yet I feel a heady thrill
To see the white rice in the air
Blown every which way round the square
Before the *Winter Palace*. Cold
Grey sky sets off the flourished gold
And whipped-cream plaster rococo
Embellishments that help to make
The place look such a birthday cake –
I only wish there were more snow.
Despite the risk of frozen feet
I'd like to see the dream complete.

2

Speaking of feet: they're killing me.
I've walked around the city now
For ages, there's so much to see.
Already I can well see how
Poets, composers, every kind
Of artist thought this town designed
Exclusively so that they might
Be stimulated day and night
To works of genius. I shan't
Pretend to be quite in their league.
Indeed I'd rather plead fatigue
And shirk the challenge, but I can't:
The ghosts of all those gifted men
Are sneering as I suck my pen.

continued

3

The greatest of them all, of course,
Was *Pushkin*. I'm just halfway through
His masterpiece, but the full force
Of Inspiration's only too
Apparent. In all literature
There's no fecundity so pure
As his. Through him the Gods gave tongue
And made damned certain he died young.
So multifarious a voice,
So disciplined a formal sense -
His talent was just too immense.
He had to go. There was no choice.
Like *Mozart* he was *Heaven*-sent
And back to *Heaven* he soon went.

4

'*Eugene Onegin*'! In an hour
I read one stanza. Such compression
Demands all one's attentive power.
Besides, I must make a confession:
My *Russian*, after months of sweat,
Is really not so hot as yet.
In fact it's pretty poor. As well
As being envious as *Hell*
Of all your other attributes,
I wish my Army hitch had taught
Me tricks of a more taxing sort.
I studied how to polish boots
With spit and spoon. *You* got to know
The lingo of the dreaded foe.

5

We neither of us won the war.
I'm told it sort of went away
When both sides settled for a draw.
Lord Chalfont still has lots to say
About the imminent Red Threat,

But nothing much has happened yet
In global terms. The *Warsaw Pact*
Intractably remains a fact.
It's hard to see how they could lose,
Our experts warn, should they advance.
Poor NATO wouldn't stand a chance.
They've got more tanks than they can use.
By midday on *D-Day Plus One*
They'd be in *Budleigh Salterton.*

6

But will they risk annihilation?
I don't think anybody knows.
The thought of total devastation
If ever harsh words come to blows
Still keeps the Super-powers in check.
Better to wring each other's neck
At second hand, on battlegrounds
Where losses can be kept in bounds.
When Ideologies collide
They tend to choose exotic places
Where folk with ethnic-looking faces
Don't mind committing suicide,
Or anyway don't seem to. Thus
It's all thrashed out without much fuss.

7

Meanwhile the vast *USSR*
Grows ever stronger and more bored.
The Ceaseless Struggle rages far
Away, in little lands abroad.
The *Marxist-Leninist* ideal
At home long since became as real
As it could ever be. The State
Takes charge of everybody's fate
From womb to tomb. Complete control
Is exercised on all resources.

continued

The harnessing of natural forces
By now includes the human soul.
What you may do or even dream
Is all laid down by the Régime,

8

Which should have no more use for Terror.
The People now are too well drilled
To contemplate embracing error.
Assent's so thoroughly instilled
That new directives are obeyed
Before they've even been displayed
On all those billboards and red flags
Beneath which every building sags.
Nobody sane could see the need
For harsher methods than this thick
Miasma of bad rhetoric.
The Masses long ago agreed
That Inner Freedom makes no sense.
Which only leaves the Dissidents -

9

Who go through several kinds of *Hell*
In special clinics where the drugs
That make them ill instead of well
Are forced upon them, not by thugs,
But qualified psychiatrists.
It's one of History's little twists:
The sane are classified insane
And rather than relieving pain
The doctors cause it. Strange, but true -
When those with preternatural guts
Are first of all defined as nuts,
Then made so - but that's *Marx* for you:
To put the Future beyond doubt
What must be must be brought about.

10

The common run of folk, meanwhile,
Can feel comparatively safe
From decimation *Stalin*-style.
Their bonds, though still strong, do not chafe
As proudly they with one accord
March asymptotically toward
That feast of dubious delights
Zinoviev calls the Yawning Heights -
A Workers' Paradise on Earth
Which has no use for abstract thought.
Fantastically good at sport
A new Mankind has come to birth,
A race that stands a whole head taller -
Except the head's a trifle smaller.

11

Useless to ask what might have been
Had things stayed roughly as they were.
October 1917
Made certain nothing could occur
Save transformation. History's tide -
Which *Spengler* said we have to ride
Or else go under - ran its course
With hypermetamorphic force
Until no links were left to sever.
All ties were broken with the past.
No going back. The die was cast
And everything was changed forever.
How strange, in that case, we should feel
Those days to be so much more real

12

Than these. Yet really not so strange,
For nothing dates like human dreams
Of *Heaven*. Terrified of change,

continued

The *Russia* of the present seems
An embolism. Time forgot
To flow, and stopped, and formed a clot.
There's next to nowt in the whole place –
Including rockets aimed at Space –
That wouldn't be there anyway
Had *Lenin* failed to catch his train.
Suppose he'd chosen to remain
In *Zurich*, who can really say
His country would not now be strong?
Perhaps he got the whole thing wrong

13

And simply blasted in the bud
What might have been a brilliant flower.
Perhaps in shedding so much blood
To gain unchallengeable power
He stopped what was just getting started
And left his country broken-hearted,
With what result we now all know –
The *Gulag Archipelago*.
Too black a thought with which to end
This letter, and besides, I'm too
Aware that I'm addressing *you* –
A master of the light touch. Friend,
Forgive my solemn voice of doom.
I aimed at gaiety, not gloom,

14

But somehow lost my mirth. Mistake.
It's boorish to parade one's grief
And weep for a whole country's sake,
Assuming it's lost all belief
In human decency. The fact
Remains that, though the deck is stacked
Against them, none the less the just
Are born and win each other's trust.

Nadezhda Mandelstam has said
The truth still comes back from the grave
And she should know. I think I'll waive
What rights I have to mourn the dead.
I'm better at the kind of tears
I cried when seeing '*Donkey's Years*'.

15

Besides I like it here. I've seen
The *Peter-Paul* and the *Tsars'* tombs.
I've stared at the *Bronze Horseman*, been
Through all the *Hermitage*'s rooms.
I've seen the Empress *Catherine*'s clock -
A ten-foot wingspan gold peacock
Some Grand Duke thought the kind of gift
That might convey his general drift.
I've seen . . . But there seems little point,
Here in this Window on the West,
In telling you what you know best.
You've been here and you've cased the joint,
Liking to know whereof you speak.
Good principle. See you next week.

Clive James

Angel Hill

A sailor came walking down Angel Hill,
He knocked on my door with a right good will,
With a right good will he knocked on my door.
He said, 'My friend, we have met before.'
    No, never, said I.

continued

55

He searched my eye with a sea-blue stare
And he laughed aloud on the Cornish air,
On the Cornish air he laughed aloud
And he said, 'My friend, you have grown too proud.'
    No, never, said I.

'In war we swallowed the bitter bread
And drank of the brine,' the sailor said.
'We took of the bread and we tasted the brine
As I bound your wounds and you bound mine.'
    No, never, said I.

'By day and night on the diving sea
We whistled to sun and moon,' said he.
'Together we whistled to moon and sun
And vowed our stars should be as one.'
    No, never, said I.

'And now,' he said, 'that the war is past
I come to your hearth and home at last.
I come to your home and hearth to share
Whatever fortune waits me there.'
    No, never, said I.

'I have no wife nor son,' he said,
'Nor pillow on which to lay my head,
No pillow have I, nor wife nor son,
Till you shall give to me my own.'
    No, never, said I.

His eye it flashed like a lightning-dart
And still as a stone then stood my heart.
My heart as a granite stone was still
And he said, 'My friend, but I think you will.'
    No, never, said I.

The sailor smiled and turned in his track
And shifted the bundle on his back
And I heard him sing as he strolled away,
'You'll send and you'll fetch me one fine day.'
    No, never, said I.

Charles Causley

Nemea

A song in the valley of Nemea:
Sing quiet, quite quiet here.

Song for the brides of Argos
Combing the swarms of golden hair:
Quite quiet, quiet there.

Under the rolling comb of grass,
The sword outrusts the golden helm.

Agamemnon under tumulus serene
Outsmiles the jury of skeletons:
Cool under cumulus the lion queen:

Only the drum can celebrate,
Only the adjective outlive them.

A song in the valley of Nemea:
Sing quiet, quiet, quiet here.

Tone of the frog in the empty well,
Drone of the bald bee on the cold skull,

Quiet, Quiet, Quiet.

Lawrence Durrell

Lament

When I was a windy boy and a bit
And the black spit of the chapel fold,
(Sighed the old ram rod, dying of women),
I tiptoed shy in the gooseberry wood,
The rude owl cried like a telltale tit,
I skipped in a blush as the big girls rolled
Ninepin down on the donkeys' common,
And on seesaw sunday nights I wooed
Whoever I would with my wicked eyes,
The whole of the moon I could love and leave
All the green leaved little weddings' wives
In the coal black bush and let them grieve.

When I was a gusty man and a half
And the black beast of the beetles' pews,
(Sighed the old ram rod, dying of bitches),
Not a boy and a bit in the wick-
Dipping moon and drunk as a new dropped calf,
I whistled all night in the twisted flues,
Midwives grew in the midnight ditches,
And the sizzling beds of the town cried, Quick! -
Whenever I dove in a breast high shoal,
Wherever I ramped in the clover quilts,
Whatsoever I did in the coal-
Black night, I left my quivering prints.

When I was a man you could call a man
And the black cross of the holy house,
(Sighed the old ram rod, dying of welcome),
Brandy and ripe in my bright, bass prime,
No springtailed tom in the red hot town
With every simmering woman his mouse
But a hillocky bull in the swelter
Of summer come in his great good time
To the sultry, biding herds, I said,
Oh, time enough when the blood creeps cold,
And I lie down but to sleep in bed,
For my sulking, skulking, coal black soul!

When I was a half of the man I was
And serve me right as the preachers warn,
(Sighed the old ram rod, dying of downfall),
No flailing calf or cat in a flame
Or hickory bull in milky grass
But a black sheep with a crumpled horn,
At last the soul from its foul mousehole
Slunk pouting out when the limp time came;
And I gave my soul a blind, slashed eye,
Gristle and rind, and a roarers' life,
And I shoved it into the coal black sky
To find a woman's soul for a wife.

Now I am a man no more no more
And a black reward for a roaring life,
(Sighed the old ram rod, dying of strangers),
Tidy and cursed in my dove cooed room
I lie down thin and hear the good bells jaw –
For, oh, my soul found a sunday wife
In the coal black sky and she bore angels!
Harpies around me out of her womb!
Chastity prays for me, piety sings,
Innocence sweetens my last black breath,
Modesty hides my thighs in her wings,
And all the deadly virtues plague my death!

Dylan Thomas

The sofas, fogs, and cinemas

I have lived it, and lived it,
My nervous, luxury civilization,
My sugar-loving nerves have battered me to pieces.

. . . Their idea of literature is hopeless.
Make them drink their own poetry!
Let them eat their gross novel, full of mud.

It's quiet; just the fresh, chilly weather . . . and he
Gets up from his dead bedroom, and comes in here
And digs himself into the sofa.
He stays there up to two hours in the hole - and talks
- Straight into the large subjects, he faces up to *everything*
It's . . . . . . damnably depressing.
(That great lavatory coat . . . the cigarillo burning
In the little dish . . . And when he calls out: 'Ha!'
Madness! - you no longer possess your own furniture.)

On my bad days (and I'm being broken
At this very moment) I speak of my ambitions . . . and he
Becomes intensely gloomy, with the look of something
   jugged,
Morose, sour, mouldering away, with lockjaw. . . .

I grow coarser; and more modern (*I*, who am driven mad
By my ideas; who go nowhere;
Who dare not leave my front door, lest an idea . . .)
All right. I admit everything, everything!

Oh yes, the opera (Ah, but the cinema)
He particularly enjoys it, enjoys it *horribly*, when someone's
   ill
At the last minute; and they specially fly in
A new, gigantic, Dutch soprano. He wants to help her
With her arias.   Old goat! Blasphemer!
He wants to help her with her arias!

No, I . . . go to the cinema,
I particularly like it when the fog is thick, the street
Is like a hole in an old coat, and the light is brown as
    laudanum.
. . . the fogs! the fogs! The cinemas
Where the criminal shadow-literature flickers over our faces,
The screen is spread out like a thundercloud - that bangs
And splashes you with acid . . . or lies derelict, with lighted
    waters in it,
And in the silence, drips and crackles - taciturn, luxurious.
. . . The drugged and battered Philistines
Are all around you in the auditorium . . .

And he . . . is somewhere else, in his dead bedroom clothes,
He wants to make me think his thoughts
And they will be *enormous*, dull - (just the sort
To keep away from).
. . . when I see that cigarillo, when I see it . . . smoking
And he wants to face the international situation . . .
Lunatic rages! Blackness! Suffocation!

- All this sitting about in cafés to calm down
Simply wears me out. And their idea of literature!
The idiotic cut of the stanzas; the novels, full up, gross.

I have lived it, and I know too much.
My café-nerves are breaking me
With black, exhausting information.

                                        Rosemary Tonks

Manhood and youth

When first the lean-flanked, cold-eyed Goddess
entered my bed, she wore the hazy face

of nameless women, hardly known, remembered
from crowded city streets, or the polite word

at an open door. Constancy enough,
for me, in her unvarying naked flesh,

those eyes whose level, blinkless glance
carried no spark of passion or intelligence.

How different now! A solitary image,
devoted, feeding children, showing age,

she questions me, her eyes aflame with needs
clarified at death-beds and on birth-beds.

And I, beside her sleep, and in her kitchen,
beloved, approved, indulged – a sombre man,

from phantasies of power, and sleights of will,
am brought at last to face the terrible

incarnation forced of things that are:
the Goddess as a chosen fellow creature.

Whom I must live with till my life is ended;
husband and master, mortal and afraid.

Tony Connor

from *Wildtrack*

The Rib

(Sonnet: to Jeanne Duval)

Honey and feathers, silk of the inside lip,
thick breath, hot heart, blind trembling at the knees:
her lacing fronds, his urgent slide and grip:
the sensual symphony is scored for these,

and these you gave: more still: the subtle drums,
spilt coffee on a white and starchy cloth
(through pampas grass the svelte procession comes,
the cool delicious taper claims its moth).

Only those unseen wings within him flapped
wild to be soaring in unperfumed air.
They itched beneath his skin. He paced the room,

sick with that throbbing pain: but flew nowhere.
His naked shoulders never grew a plume.
It was his lust, not yours, that held him trapped.

Hold tight for a steep dive. Bolt your
stomach into place, Jack. An insanely
intrepid dive through the steep surprising
air. Then smack into (with a plume
of spray) the salt water of our beginnings.
The bitter water that gives life. The end
of all our dreams of coolness and purity.
But first, a climb. Our dive starts from the
spindly ladders of a cosmic farce.

The day God slipped Adam a Mickey Finn!

continued

Did you ever hear tell of it?
Well, Genesis is built
round belly-laughs but this one
is a boffo. The burlesque houses
of all time echo with that roar
of helpless laughter. Grimaldi,
Little Tich, W.C. Fields, you are
made truly after the image of God. To squirt
water from your button-hole, squelch
a custard-pie right in that sober citizen's
well-shaven jowls, that's true
piety.
        No disrespect,
I like jokes myself. They help one to face
seriousness, by coming at it sidelong.
But this was *the most*! Think of it: he's
lonely, tells the Chief he needs a girl.
It's creepy in the evenings, with no one
to answer your voice, or tell you please
to make up the stove. Eden? It's no
great draw without someone along to talk to
about how nice it is.
        So the Chief
says, Yes, all right, and then
WHAM! slips him a knock-out drop. Imagine that!

Ay, thou poor ghost, we will imagine that.
That sleep of Adam's, that thick restless swoon,
that coma hung with shadows and sharp dreams,
snakes crawling down the walls, fat spiders in
the bath (look that one up in Freud, fellows),
eyes sealed by God's occluding touch, teeth clenched,
look how his hands open and shut - he wants
to fight the beasts that attack him in his dream!
Hear him keep moaning? Adam, I would not
wish such a sleep on you.
        But that's not all!

The act gets better! What a genius, this
cosmic comedian. Out of his bag
he takes a jemmy and a silken mask.
A choker round his throat, a greasy cap.
He's going in for burglary! Before our eyes
he opens up the straight man's side and takes
- you'd never guess it - one of his ribs. Yes, you
heard me! I thought I'd never stop laughing. The
theatre was shaking, even the usherettes
couldn't stop watching the show. Why, I'd
go crazy if I had to watch the act
again. It was *too much.*
                              He takes this rib -
now look, ask anybody, don't believe me -
and says to him (still lying there asleep)
'You asked for it,' he says, 'you poor bastard' (or
something like that) and getting out some tools
and welding equipment, right there before our eyes
he makes it into a WOMAN!
                              Well, you can
imagine how that brought the house down. I can
still hear the way they clapped and cheered. Well, I mean!
Conjuring on top of an act like that!
'Okay,' he says, 'it's all
over', and the straight
man, Adam, gets up and takes a bow,
then all of a sudden he says 'Where's my
RIB!' and down comes his hand on that side - 'Hey!
Come back here! I'm a rib short!' Laugh? They
started again, till I thought they'd die. Honest!
I'll give him that, this Adam was quite
good in the part. I mean, he made it live.
'Where's that rib?' he says again, and 'Help!'
Just as if anybody could
help him! So of course everyone laughed
again. And *then* - just picture it! - he comes
slap face to face with this babe!

continued

Well, after that the band just had to start
playing and the stage was cleared
for the performing seals.

What else?
A trouper knows when an act reaches its
natural finish. No one could laugh any more. I found
tears on my face. That's how hard I'd been
either laughing, or something.
Well, I *mean* . .

(*Post-operational*)
His eyelids opened. Light hammered on his nerves.
The tall grass heaved, with fever or desire.
The garden rocked him with its gentle curves.

The loneliness that coiled its rusty wire
about his heart, had parted. He was free.
Love shimmered like the air above a fire.

This was the miracle that had to be.
Naked, confiding, near enough to touch,
motionless in the moving light stood she.

Was he not blest beyond analysis?
His body had no doubts: its good was here:
and, dolphin-jumping in those waves of bliss,

worshipped the moon that burned so hard and clear,
worshipped the tides that made the waters dance.
O gentle earth! O crystal atmosphere!

Yet there was fear within his avid glance.

John Wain

66

Self's the man

Oh, no one can deny
That Arnold is less selfish than I.
He married a woman to stop her getting away
Now she's there all day,

And the money he gets for wasting his life on work
She takes as her perk
To pay for the kiddies' clobber and the drier
And the electric fire,

And when he finishes supper
Planning to have a read at the evening paper
Its *Put a screw in this wall* -
He has no time at all,

With the nippers to wheel round the houses
And the hall to paint in his old trousers
And that letter to her mother
Saying *Won't you come for the summer.*

To compare his life and mine
Makes me feel a swine:
Oh, no one can deny
That Arnold is less selfish than I.

But wait, not so fast:
Is there such a contrast?
He was out for his own ends
Not just pleasing his friends;

And if it was such a mistake
He still did it for his own sake,
Playing his own game.
So he and I are the same,

Only I'm better hand
At knowing what I can stand
Without them sending a van -
Or I suppose I can.

Philip Larkin

A common interest

What is needed is a common interest,
What you might call a friendly rivalry.

My wife is patron of the cat,
I am patron of the dog.
The cat and the dog are not exactly friends,
In fact they lead a rather turbulent life.

My wife backs the cat and I support the dog.
She fattens the cat and keeps its claws in trim,
I teach the dog a trick or two.

She has equipped her client with sparklers
To brandish in its mouth.
I tell her, Peace Prizes have come from gunpowder.
We laugh. Then I teach my protégé to spit.

An atomic pellet placed in the cat's saucer?
We discuss it sensibly, and agree
To avoid any serious damage to the house.
After all, we live in it.

I think she is training the cat to drop things
From a height.
I shall fit the dog out with a helmet
And file its teeth.

How the fur flies!

We live in perfect amity, my wife and I,
Our marriage is founded on a rock.

D. J. Enright

Spirit level

for George and Sue, in New Guinea

An odd gift, certainly. One
Would have to be hard up
To give such a thing for a wedding.
A plate or a cup

Of Eighteenth Century pot
Rustic, of course,
Embellished with two seated lovers
And a grazing horse;

Or else a spied treasure of bronze
From Samarkand -
A perfectionist's quodlibet
From a shop on the Strand -

Ah, these would be elegant gifts,
And would surely raise
The naked Papuans to envy
The White Man's ways.

I wish I had thought of them sooner,
Or luck had slunk
To the wellnigh miraculous gift
In a shopful of junk.

But my eye has domiciled with this
Uncompromising wood,
Its brass fittings inelegant,
Its proportions crude.

Drab product of a technology
That has left it behind,
A tool mass-produced without passion
Of body or mind . . .

continued

But through its windows the small, oblong
Bubble of oil
- Wherever you are, on English
Or New Guinean soil -

Still keeps its strange relationship
To the round earth
And points to the perfect tangent
Of its spheroid girth.

The awe-inspiring simplicity
Of that design
Makes irrelevant lack of grace
And brutal line.

Such is my emblem for how I honour you,
For what I give
Comes from the responding eye
Where all truths live.

I pray for you through this emblem
That each of you in each,
The straight wood, the bubble of oil,
True centre reach,

And right-angled with the world,
Hold its full sphere
With the delicate poise
Of the hoof of a deer.

Anthony Conran

Testament

Pure melody, love without alteration,
Flame without smoke, cresses from a clean brook,
The sun and moon as it were casting dice
With ample falls of rain,
Then comes the peaceful moment of appraisal,
The first and last lines of our testament,
With you ensconced high in the castle turret,
Combing your dark hair at a silver mirror,
And me below, sharpening my quill again.

This body is now yours; therefore I own it.
Your body is now mine; therefore you own it.
As for our single heart, let it stay ours
Since neither may disown it
While still it flowers in the same dream of flowers.

Robert Graves

I leave this at your ear
(for Nessie Dunsmuir)

I leave this at your ear for when you wake,
A creature in its abstract cage asleep.
Your dreams blindfold you by the light they make.

The owl called from the naked-woman tree
As I came down by the Kyle farm to hear
Your house silent by the speaking sea.

I have come late but I have come before
Later with slaked steps from stone to stone
To hope to find you listening for the door.

I stand in the ticking room. My dear, I take
A moth kiss from your breath. The shore gulls cry.
I leave this at your ear for when you wake.

W.S. Graham

71

Song of the October wind

A mighty air-sea, fierce and very clean,
Was gliding in across the city.
Oxygenating gusts swept down and
Chloroformed us, in a light too bright to see by.

On pavements - china and milk pages
In a good book, freshly iced by the printing press -
October flash-floated. And you and I were moving
With alert, sane, and possessive steps. At home,

My sofa wrote her creaking, narcoleptic's Iliad.
My bathroom drank the Styx (bathwater
Of the Underworld). My telephone took all its voices
And gave them to the Furies, to practise with.

While slowly - to gigantic, muddy blows of music
From a pestle and mortar - roof, floor, walls, doors,
My London, stuffed with whisky-dark hotels,
Began to pant like a great ode!

And threw, carelessly, into our veins
Information - all the things we needed to know,
For which there are no words, *not even thoughts*.
And this was an ode shaken from a box of rats.

The first sky from October's aviary
Of bone-dry, thudding skies, joyful, free, and young,
With its wings lifted our souls, heavy as cities,
Effortlessly. We were trustworthy again.

Ritz, Savoy, Claridge's, hotels full of peacock words,
Were beaten white by Boreas; and as
Electric frosts scratched the windows
Fitting in their awkward childish pane of glowing stone,

We - copied the foaming *with our souls*!
The same ode tore the streets inside us. And lit
Catwalks, sofas, taxis in that city with a light
So bright, even the blind could see by it.

Rosemary Tonks

Dark August

So much rain, so much life like the swollen sky
of this black August. My sister, the sun,
broods in her yellow room and won't come out.

Everything goes to hell; the mountains fume
like a kettle, rivers over-run, still,
she will not rise and turn off the rain.

She's in her room, fondling old things,
my poems, turning her album. Even if thunder falls
like a crash of plates from the sky,

she does not come out.
Don't you know I love you but am hopeless
at fixing the rain? But I am learning slowly

to love the dark days, the steaming hills,
the air with gossiping mosquitoes,
and to sip the medicine of bitterness,

so that when you emerge, my sister,
parting the beads of the rain,
with your forehead of flowers and eyes of forgiveness,

all will not be as it was, but it will be true,
(you see they will not let me love
as I want), because my sister, then

I would have learnt to love black days like bright ones,
the black rain, the white hills, when once
I loved only my happiness and you.

Derek Walcott

Party piece

He said:

'Let's stay here
Now this place has emptied
And make gentle pornography with one another,
While the partygoers go out
And the dawn creeps in,
Like a stranger.

'Let us not hesitate
Over what we know
Or over how cold this place has become,
But lets unclip our minds
And let tumble free
The mad, mangled crocodile of love.'

So they did,
There among the woodbines and guinness stains,
And later he caught a bus and she a train
And all there was between them then
was rain.

Brian Patten

Reasons for attendance

The trumpet's voice, loud and authoritative,
Draws me a moment to the lighted glass
To watch the dancers - all under twenty-five -
Shifting intently, face to flushed face,
Solemnly on the beat of happiness.

- Or so I fancy, sensing the smoke and sweat,
The wonderful feel of girls. Why be out here?
But then, why be in there? Sex, yes, but what
Is sex? Surely, to think the lion's share
Of happiness is found by couples - sheer

Inaccuracy, as far as I'm concerned.
What calls me is that lifted, rough-tongued bell
(Art, if you like) whose individual sound
Insists I too am individual.
It speaks; I hear; others may hear as well,

But not for me, nor I for them; and so
With happiness. Therefore I stay outside,
Believing this; and they maul to and fro,
Believing that; and both are satisfied,
If no one has misjudged himself. Or lied.

Philip Larkin

Odd

In front of our house in Golders Green
the lawn, like a cliché, mutters 'Rose bushes.'
The whole suburb is very respectable.
Ugly men drive past in funeral suits,
from their necks you can tell they're overweight.

Sodium lamp-posts, at night, hose empty roads
with gold which treacles over pavement trees,
polishes brittle hedges, clings on closed, parked cars.
If a light should fly on in an upstairs room
odds on two someones are going to sleep.

It's unusual to meet a beggar,
you hardly ever see a someone drunk.
It's a nice, clean, quiet, religious place.
For my part, now and then, I want to scream:
thus, by the neighbours, am considered odd.

From the sensible wastes of Golders Green
I journey to Soho where a job owns me.
Soho is not a respectable place.
Underweight women in the gamiest of skirts
bleed a smile of false teeth at ugly men.

Later, the dark is shabby with paste electric
of peeporamas, brothels, clubs and pubs,
restaurants that sport sallow waiters who cough.
If a light should fly on in an upstairs room
odds on two someones are going to bed.

It's customary to see many beggars,
common to meet people roaring and drunk.
It's a nice, loud, dirty, irreligious place.
For my part, now and then, I want to scream:
thus, by Soho friends, am considered odd.

Dannie Abse

Hold-up

The lights were red, refused to change,
Ash-ends grew longer, no one spoke,
The papers faded in their hands,
The bubbles in the football pools
Went flat, the hot news froze, the dates
They could not keep were dropped like charred
Matches, the girls no longer flagged
Their sex, besides the code was lost,
The engine stalled, a tall glass box
On the pavement held a corpse in pickle
His ear still cocked, and no one spoke,
No number rang, for miles behind
The other buses nudged and blared
And no one dared get out. The conductress
Was dark and lost, refused to change.

Louis MacNeice

Address not known

So you are gone, and are proved bad change, as we had
   always known,
And I am left in London the metropolitan city,
Perhaps to twist this incident into a durable poem –
The lesson of those who give their love to phenomenal
   beauty.

I am coming to think now that all I have loved were
   shadows
Strayed up from a dead world, through a gap in a raped
   tomb,
Or where the narcissus battens in mythological meadows:
Your face was painted upon the coffin-lid from Fayoum.

continued

Is this my pain that is speaking? The pain was not long
  protracted:
I make a statement, forgive the betrayal, the meanness, the
  theft.
Human, I cannot suppose you had planned all that was
  enacted:
Fortitude must be procured to encounter the hollowness left.

The sun will not haver in its course for the lack of you,
Nor the flowers fail in colour, nor the bird stint in its song.
Only the heart that wanted somehow to have opened up
Finds the frost in the day's air, and the nights which appear
  too long.

John Heath-Stubbs

Anecdote of 2 a.m.

'Why was she lost?' my darling said aloud
With never a movement in her sleep. I lay
Awake and watched her breathe, remote and proud.

Her words reached out where I could never be.
She dreamed a world remote from all I was.
'Why was she lost?' She was not asking me.

I knew that there was nothing I could say.
She breathed and dreamed beyond our kisses' sphere.
My watchful night was her unconscious day.

I could not tell what dreams disturbed her heart.
She spoke, and never knew my tongue was tied.
I longed to bless her but she lay apart.

That was our last night, if I could have known.
But I remember still how in the dark
She dreamed her question and we lay alone.

John Wain

78

Endings

Things do not explode
they fail, they fade,

as sunlight fades from the flesh
as the foam drains quick in the sand,

even love's lightning flash
has no thunderous end,

it dies with the sound
of flowers fading like the flesh

from sweating pumice stone,
everything shapes this

till we are left
with the silence that surrounds Beethoven's head.

Derek Walcott

She tells her love while half asleep

She tells her love while half asleep,
  In the dark hours,
    With half-words whispered low:
As Earth stirs in her winter sleep
  And puts out grass and flowers
    Despite the snow,
    Despite the falling snow.

Robert Graves

Witches

Once was every woman the witch
To ride a weed the ragwort road;
Devil to do whatever she would:
Each rosebud, every old bitch.

Did they bargain their bodies or no?
Proprietary the devil that
Went horsing on their every thought
When they scowled the strong and lucky low.

Dancing in Ireland nightly, gone
To Norway (the ploughboy bridled),
Nightlong under the blackamoor spraddled,
Back beside their spouse by dawn.

As if they had dreamed all. Did they dream it?
Oh, our science says they did.
It was all wishfully dreamed in bed.
Small psychology would unseam it.

Bitches still sulk, rosebuds blow,
And we are devilled. And though these weep
Over our harms, who's to know
Where their feet dance while their heads sleep?

Ted Hughes

Love after love

The time will come
when, with elation,
you will greet yourself arriving
at your own door, in your own mirror,
and each will smile at the other's welcome,

and say sit here. Eat.
You will love again the stranger who was your self.
Give wine. Give bread. Give back your heart
to itself, to the stranger who has loved you

all your life, whom you ignored
for another, who knows you by heart.
Take down the love-letters from the bookshelf

the photographs, the desperate notes,
peel your own image from the mirror.
Sit. Feast on your life.

Derek Walcott

Days

What are days for?
Days are where we live.
They come, they wake us
Time and time over.
They are to be happy in:
Where can we live but days?

Ah, solving that question
Brings the priest and the doctor
In their long coats
Running over the fields.

Philip Larkin

Haloes

Of course haloes are out of fashion.
The commissar is in the castle,
the haemophylic king plays golf
in exile. Feudal days, no more.
Once martyrs were a glut on the market,
now famine faces sink in Asia;
now lamps switched on in drawing rooms
reveal suffering saints no longer there -
as if they had leapt down from walls
leaving behind them halo-tissue.

Such a round shining on walls!
Such a bleeding of intense light!
And all those haloes in hymns of paint,
in museums, in galleries, counterfeit.
Still we appease the old deities –
else we would be like madmen laughing
in public buildings, apparent joy
where rational people speak in whispers;
else saints would never look so ecstatic
in chiaroscuro, on starvation diet.

The Pope does not eat his own entrails
with a golden fork, nor his secretary
cease from phoning the Stock Exchange.
Haloes set men alight in Prague.
Here crowds prefer to shout, 'Easy, Easy,'
at a poisoned green pitch in floodlight.
Pop star, film star, space man, gangster,
move smilingly from camera to camera
seldom to become ritual torches.
Each worth a million, say the guides.

Rightly we are suspicious of haloes
and heroes, of thorns and royal tiaras.
Day and night, an H-bomb circles the world
and Fatty and his henchmen walk
on marble floors, their heritage.
No wonder important men lift up
their hats politely, revealing bald heads.
No-one minds. Their skins have healed.
Think of wall lamps switched off
savagely, all haloes fleeing.

Dannie Abse

The shield of Achilles

She looked over his shoulder
  For vines and olive trees,
Marble well-governed cities
  And ships upon untamed seas,
But there on the shining metal
  His hands had put instead
An artificial wilderness
  And a sky like lead.

A plain without a feature, bare and brown,
  No blade of grass, no sign of neighbourhood,
Nothing to eat and nowhere to sit down,
  Yet, congregated on its blankness, stood
  An unintelligible multitude.
A million eyes, a million boots in line,
Without expression, waiting for a sign.

Out of the air a voice without a face
  Proved by statistics that some cause was just
In tones as dry and level as the place:
  No one was cheered and nothing was discussed;
  Column by column in a cloud of dust
They marched away enduring a belief
Whose logic brought them, somewhere else, to grief.

She looked over his shoulder
  For ritual pieties,
White flower-garlanded heifers,
  Libation and sacrifice,
But there on the shining metal
  Where the altar should have been,
She saw by his flickering forge-light
  Quite another scene.

Barbed wire enclosed an arbitrary spot
　　Where bored officials lounged (one cracked a joke)
And sentries sweated for the day was hot:
　　A crowd of ordinary decent folk
　　Watched from without and neither moved nor spoke
As three pale figures were led forth and bound
To three posts driven upright in the ground.

The mass and majesty of this world, all
　　That carries weight and always weighs the same
Lay in the hands of others; they were small
　　And could not hope for help and no help came:
　　What their foes liked to do was done, their shame
Was all the worst could wish; they lost their pride
And died as men before their bodies died.

She looked over his shoulder
　　For athletes at their games,
Men and women in a dance
　　Moving their sweet limbs
Quick, quick, to music,
　　But there on the shining shield
His hands had set no dancing-floor
　　But a weed-choked field.

A ragged urchin, aimless and alone,
　　Loitered about that vacancy, a bird
Flew up to safety from his well-aimed stone:
　　That girls are raped, that two boys knife a third,
　　Were axioms to him, who'd never heard
Of any world where promises were kept,
Or one could weep because another wept.

The thin-lipped armourer,
　　Hephaestos hobbled away,
Thetis of the shining breasts
　　Cried out in dismay
At what the god had wrought
　　To please her son, the strong
Iron-hearted man-slaying Achilles
　　Who would not live long.

W.H. Auden

Kneeling

Moments of great calm,
Kneeling before an altar
Of wood in a stone church
In summer, waiting for the God
To speak; the air a staircase
For silence; the sun's light
Ringing me, as though I acted
A great rôle. And the audiences
Still; all that close throng
Of spirits waiting, as I,
For the message.
                    Prompt me, God;
But not yet. When I speak,
Though it be you who speak
Through me, something is lost.
The meaning is in the waiting.

R.S. Thomas

Before the anœsthetic,
or
A real fright

Intolerably sad, profound
St. Giles's bells are ringing round,
They bring the slanting summer rain
To tap the chestnut boughs again
Whose shadowy cave of rainy leaves
The gusty belfry-song receives.
Intolerably sad and true,
Victorian red and jewel* blue,

* Adjective from Rumer Godden.

The mellow bells are ringing round
And charge the evening light with sound,
And I look motionless from bed
On heavy trees and purple red
And hear the midland bricks and tiles
Throw back the bells of stone St. Giles,
Bells, ancient now as castle walls,
Now hard and new as pitchpine stalls,
Now full with help from ages past,
Now dull with death and hell at last.
Swing up! and give me hope of life,
Swing down! and plunge the surgeon's knife.
I, breathing for a moment, see
Death wing himself away from me
And think, as on this bed I lie,
Is it extinction when I die?
I move my limbs and use my sight;
Not yet, thank God, not yet the Night.
Oh better far those echoing hells
Half-threaten'd in the pealing bells
Than that this 'I' should cease to be –
Come quickly, Lord, come quick to me.
St. Giles's bells are asking now
'And hast thou known the Lord, hast thou?'
St. Giles's bells, they richly ring
'And was that Lord our Christ the King?'
St. Giles's bells they hear me call
I never knew the Lord at all.
Oh not in me your Saviour dwells
You ancient, rich St. Giles's bells.
Illuminated missals – spires –
Wide screens and decorated quires –
All these I loved, and on my knees
I thanked myself for knowing these
And watched the morning sunlight pass
Through richly stained Victorian glass
And in the colour-shafted air
I, kneeling, thought the Lord was there.
Now, lying in the gathering mist
I know that Lord did not exist;

Now, lest this 'I' should cease to be,
Come, real Lord, come quick to me.
With every gust the chestnut sighs,
With every breath, a mortal dies;
The man who smiled alone, alone,
And went his journey on his own
With 'Will you give my wife this letter,
In case, of course, I don't get better?'
Waits for his coffin lid to close
On waxen head and yellow toes.
Almighty Saviour, had I Faith
There'd be no fight with kindly Death.
Intolerably long and deep
St. Giles's bells swing on in sleep:
'But still you go from here alone'
Say all the bells about the Throne.

John Betjeman

The moor

It was like a church to me.
I entered it on soft foot,
Breath held like a cap in the hand.
It was quiet.
What God was there made himself felt,
Not listened to, in clean colours
That brought a moistening of the eye,
In movement of the wind over grass.

There were no prayers said. But stillness
Of the heart's passions - that was praise
Enough; and the mind's cession
Of its kingdom. I walked on,
Simple and poor, while the air crumbled
And broke on me generously as bread.

R.S. Thomas

Growing, flying, happening

Say the soft bird's name, but do not be surprised
to see it fall
headlong, struck skyless, into its pigeonhole –
columba palumbus and you have it dead,
wedged, neat, unwinged in your head.

That that black-backed tatter-winged thing
straking the harbour water and then plummeting
down, to come up, sleek head-a-cock,
a minted herring shining in its beak,
is a *guillemot*, is neither here nor there
in the amazement of its rising,
wings slicing the stiff salt air.

That of that spindling spear-leaved plant,
wearing the palest purple umbel,
many-headed, blue-tinted, stilt-stalked
at the stream-edge, one should say briefly
angelica, is by-the-way (though grant
the name itself to be beautiful).
Grant too that any name
makes its own music, that *bryony, sally-my-handsome*
burst at their sound into flower,
and that *falcon* and *phalarope* fly off in the ear,
still,
names are for saying at home.

The point is seeing – the grace
beyond recognition, the ways
of the bird rising, unnamed, unknown,
beyond the range of language, beyond its noun.
Eyes open on growing, flying, happening,
and go on opening. Manifold, the world
dawns on unrecognising, realising eyes.
Amazement is the thing.
Not love, but the astonishment of loving.

Alastair Reid

Earth

Let the day grow on you upward
through your feet
the vegetal knuckles

to your knees of stone,
until by evening you are a black tree;
feel, with evening,

the swifts thicken your hair,
the new moon rising out of your forehead,
and the moonlit veins of silver

running from your armpits
like rivulets under white leaves.
Sleep, as ants

cross over your eyelids.
You have never possessed anything
as deeply as this.

This is all you have owned
from the first outcry
through forever;

you can never be dispossessed.

Derek Walcott

Music on the moon

The pianos on the moon are so long
The pianist's hand must be fifteen fingers strong.

The violins on the moon are so violent
They have to be sunk in deep wells, and then they only seem
   to be silent.

The bassoons on the moon blow no notes
But huge blue loons that flap slowly away with undulating
   throats.

Now harmonicas on the moon are humorous,
The tunes produce German Measles, but the speckles more
   numerous.

Of a trumpet on the moon you can never hear enough
Because it puffs the trumpeter up like a balloon and he
   floats off.

Double basses on the moon are a risk all right,
At the first note enormous black hands appear and carry
   away everything in sight.

Even a triangle on the moon is risky,
One ping - and there's your head a half bottle of Irish
   whisky.

In the same way, be careful with the flute -
Because wherever he is, your father will find himself
   converted into a disgusting old boot.

On the whole it's best to stick to the moon's drums.
Whatever damage they do is so far off in space the news
   never comes.

Ted Hughes

Moon landing

It's natural the Boys should whoop it up for
so huge a phallic triumph, an adventure
   it would not have occurred to women
   to think worth while, made possible only

because we like huddling in gangs and knowing
the exact time: yes, our sex may in fairness
   hurrah the deed, although the motives
   that primed it were somewhat less than *menschlich*.

A grand gesture. But what does it period?
What does it osse? We were always adroiter
   with objects than lives, and more facile
   at courage than kindness: from the moment

the first flint was flaked this landing was merely
a matter of time. But our selves, like Adam's,
   still don't fit us exactly, modern
   Only in this - our lack of decorum.

Homer's heroes were certainly no braver
than our Trio, but more fortunate: Hector
   was excused the insult of having
   his valor covered by television.

Worth *going* to see? I can well believe it.
Worth *seeing*? Mneh! I once rode through a desert
   and was not charmed: give me a watered
   lively garden, remote from blatherers

about the New, the von Brauns and their ilk, where
on August mornings I can count the morning
   glories, where to die has a meaning,
   and no engine can shift my perspective.

Unsmudged, thank God, my Moon still queens the Heavens
as She ebbs and fulls, a Presence to glop at,
   Her Old Man, made of grit not protein,
   still visits my Austrian several

with His old detachment, and the old warnings
still have power to scare me: Hybris comes to
   an ugly finish, Irreverence
    . is a greater oaf than Superstition.

Our apparatniks will continue making
the usual squalid mess called History:
   all we can pray for is that artists,
    chefs and saints may still appear to blithe it.

W.H. Auden

The first men on Mercury

- We come in peace from the third planet.
Would you take us to your leader?

- Bawr stretter! Bawr. Bawr. Stretterhawl?

- This is a little plastic model
of the solar system, with working parts.
You are here and we are there and we
are now here with you, is this clear?

- Gawl horrop. Bawr. Abawrhannahanna!

- Where we come from is blue and white
with brown, you see we call the brown
here 'land', the blue is 'sea', and the white
is 'clouds' over land and sea, we live
on the surface of the brown land,
all round is sea and clouds. We are 'men'.
Men come -

continued

- Glawp men! Gawrbenner menko. Menhawl?

- Men come in peace from the third planet
which we call 'earth'. We are earthmen.
Take us earthmen to your leader.

- Thmen? Thmen? Bawr. Bawrhossop.
Yuleeda tan hanna. Harrabost yuleeda.

- I am the yuleeda. You see my hands,
we carry no benner, we come in peace.
The spaceways are all stretterhawn.

- Glawn peacemen all horrabhanna tantko!
Tan come at'mstrossop. Glawp yuleeda!

- Atoms are peacegawl in our harraban
Menbat worrabost from tan hannahanna.

We know yuleeda. Go strawg backspetter quick!

- We cantantabawr, tantingko backspetter now!

- Banghapper now! Yes, third planet back.
Yuleeda will go back blue, white, brown
nowhanna! There is no more talk.

- Gawl han fasthapper?

- No. You must go back to your planet.
Go back in peace, take what you have gained
but quickly.

- Stretterworra gawl, gawl . . .

- Of course, but nothing is ever the same,
now is it? You'll remember Mercury.

Edwin Morgan

94

Resurrection

Surprised by spring,
by the green light fallen like snow
in a single evening,
by hawthorn, blackthorn, willow,
meadow - everything
woken again after how many thousand years?
As if there had been no years.

That generous throat
is a blackbird's. Now, a thrush.
And that ribbon flung out,
that silk voice, is a chaffinch's rush
to his grace-note.
Birds woo, or apportion the innocent air they're made for.
Whom do they sing for?

Old man by the river
spread out like a cross in the sun
feet bare
and stared at by three grubby children,
you've made it again, and yes we'll inherit a summer.
Always the same green clamouring fells you that wakes you.
And you have to start living again when it wakes you.

Anne Stevenson

Definition of a waterfall

Not stitched to air or water but to both
A veil hangs broken in concealing truth

And flies in vague exactitude, a dove
Born diving between rivers out of love

In drums' crescendo beat its waters grow
Conceding thunder's pianissimo

Transfixing ancient time and legend where
A future ghost streams in the present air:

From ledge to pool breakneck across rocks
Wild calm, calm chaos skein their paradox

So that excited poise is fiercely dressed
In a long instant's constant flow of rest,

So that this bridegroom and his bride in white
Parting together headlong reunite

Among her trailing braids. The inconstancy
Is reconciled to fall, falls and falls free.

John Ormond

Education of a cloud

You saw them, Sabina? Did you see them?
Yet the education of this little cloud
Full of neglect, allowed remissly so to lie
Unbrushed in some forgotten corner
Of a Monday-afternoon-in-April sky . . .

The rest abandoned it in passing by,
The swollen red-eyed country-mourners,
Unbarbered, marching on some Friday-the-thirteenth.
They knew it was not of the savage
Winter company, this tuffet for a tired cherub,

But a dear belonging of the vernal age,
Say spring, provinces of the nightingale,
Say love, the ministry of all distresses,
Say youth, Sabina, let us call it youth –

All the white capes of fancy seen afar!

Lawrence Durrell

What you should do each morning

At last it cannot matter
what openings are seen through
as long as outside any are

the same still horses, poised
against dawn, so
very white against dawn:

it does not matter
as long as shouting Yes
you rush outside

leaping on any of them then
ride madly away
singing, singing, singing.

Brian Patten

97

Considering the snail

The snail pushes through a green
night, for the grass is heavy
with water and meets over
the bright path he makes, where rain
has darkened the earth's dark. He
moves in a wood of desire,

pale antlers barely stirring
as he hunts. I cannot tell
what power is at work, drenched there
with purpose, knowing nothing.
What is a snail's fury? All
I think is that if later

I parted the blades above
the tunnel and saw the thin
trail of broken white across
litter, I would never have
imagined the slow passion
to that deliberate progress.

Thom Gunn

To paint a water lily

A green level of lily leaves
Roofs the pond's chamber and paves

The flies' furious arena: study
These, the two minds of this lady.

First observe the air's dragonfly
That eats meat, that bullets by

Or stands in space to take aim;
Others as dangerous comb the hum

Under the trees. There are battle-shouts
And death-cries everywhere hereabouts

But inaudible, so the eyes praise
To see the colours of these flies

Rainbow their arcs, spark, or settle
Cooling like beads of molten metal

Through the spectrum. Think what worse
Is the pond-bed's matter of course;

Prehistoric bedragonned times
Crawl that darkness with Latin names,

Have evolved no improvements there,
Jaws for heads, the set stare,

Ignorant of age as of hour –
Now paint the long-necked lily-flower

Which, deep in both worlds, can be still
As a painting, trembling hardly at all

Though the dragonfly alight,
Whatever horror nudge her root.

Ted Hughes

For Peter and Margaret

The wooden-shouldered tree is wild and high,
it is a plane-tree lighted inwardly,
it imprisons the sun in a cloth of leaf.
That will escape from this world though,
the tree is deliberate, it is life,
it has a musty smell and a shadow.

Bigger breasted than birds, it is breathing,
hangs with a weightless weight on everything,
having considered the sun from time to time
which vanishes in incense and yellow light:
is as silent as fog, the winter gleam
of a small sun and the birds in their flight.

It is courageous and it is alive,
this tree is nine parts of what I believe:
freedom lies in the inward of nature,
and this tree is green fire in a world of trees,
catches blue air, is neither pure nor impure,
but is alive. It is alive and dies.

Peter Levi

Snowdrop

Now is the globe shrunk tight
Round the mouse's dulled wintering heart.
Weasel and crow, as if moulded in brass,
Move through an outer darkness
Not in their right minds,
With the other deaths. She, too, pursues her ends,
Brutal as the stars of this month,
Her pale head heavy as metal.

Ted Hughes

100

Weeding

1

Here I am again with my sickle, spade, hoe
To decide over life or death, presume to call
This plant a 'weed', that one a 'flower',
Adam's prerogative, hereditary power
I can't renounce. And yet I know, I know,
It is a single generator drives them all,
And drives my murderous, my ordering hand.

These foxgloves, these red poppies, I let them stand,
Though I did not sow them. Slash the fruit-bearing bramble,
Dig out ground elder, bindweed, stinging nettle,
Real rivals, invaders whose roots ramble,
Robbing or strangling those of more delicate plants.
Or perhaps it's their strength, putting me on my mettle
To fight them for space, resist their advance.

2

I stop. I drop the spade,
Mop my face, consider:
Who's overrun the earth
And almost outrun it?
Who'll make it run out?
Who bores and guts it,
Pollutes and mutates it,
Corrodes and explodes it?
Each leaf that I laid
On the soil will feed it,
Turning death into birth.
If the cycle is breaking
Who brought it about?

continued

3

I shall go again to the overgrown plot
With my sickle, hoe, spade,
But use no weedkiller, however selective,
No chemicals, no machine.
Already the nettles, ground elder, bindweed
Spring up again.
It's a good fight, as long as neither wins,
There are fruit to pick, unpoisoned,
Weeds to look at. I call them 'wildflowers'.

Michael Hamburger

Augury

The fish faced into the current,
Its mouth agape,
Its whole head opened like a valve.
You said 'It's diseased.'

A pale crusted sore
Turned like a coin
And wound to the bottom
Unsettling silt off a weed.

We hang charmed
On the trembling catwalk:
What can fend us now
Can soothe the hurt eye

Of the sun,
Unpoison great lakes,
Turn back
The rat on the road.

Seamus Heaney

To the mermaid at Zennor

Half fish, half fallen angel, none of you
Human at all - cease your lust's
Cold and insatiate crying from the tangled bay;
Nor, sea-hag, here
Stretch webbed and skinny fingers for your prey.

This is a hideous and a wicked country,
Sloping to hateful sunsets and the end of time,
Hollow with mine-shafts, naked with granite, fanatic
With sorrow. Abortions of the past
Hop through these bogs; black-faced, the villagers
Remember burnings by the hewn stones.

Only the saints,
Drifting on oak-leaves over the Irish Sea,
To sing like pipits from their crannied cells
With a thin stream of praise; who hear the Jennifer
Sob for her sins in a purgatory of foam -
Only these holy men
Can send you slithering from the chancel steps,
And wriggling back to your sunken paradise
Among the hollow-eyed and the capsized.

John Heath-Stubbs

Going, going

I thought it would last my time -
The sense that, beyond the town,
There would always be fields and farms,
Where the village louts could climb
Such trees as were not cut down;
I knew there'd be false alarms

In the papers about old streets
And split-level shopping, but some
Have always been left so far;
And when the old parts retreat
As the bleak high-risers come
We can always escape in the car.

Things are tougher than we are, just
As earth will always respond
However we mess it about;
Chuck filth in the sea, if you must:
The tides will be clean beyond.
- But what do I feel now? Doubt?

Or age, simply? The crowd
Is young in the M1 café;
Their kids are screaming for more -
More houses, more parking allowed,
More caravan sites, more pay.
On the Business Page, a score

Of spectacled grins approve
Some takeover bid that entails
Five per cent profit (and ten
Per cent more in the estuaries): move
Your works to the unspoilt dales
(Grey area grants)! And when

You try to get near the sea
In summer . . .
                        It seems, just now,
To be happening so very fast;
Despite all the land left free
For the first time I feel somehow
That it isn't going to last,

That before I snuff it, the whole
Boiling will be bricked in
Except for the tourist parts -
First slum of Europe: a role
It won't be so hard to win,
With a cast of crooks and tarts.

And that will be England gone,
The shadows, the meadows, the lanes,
The guildhalls, the carved choirs.
There'll be books; it will linger on
In galleries; but all that remains
For us will be concrete and tyres.

Most things are never meant.
This won't be, most likely: but greeds
And garbage are too thick-strewn
To be swept up now, or invent
Excuses that make them all needs.
I just think it will happen, soon.

Philip Larkin

Hertfordshire

I had forgotten Hertfordshire,
    The large unwelcome fields of roots
Where with my knickerbockered sire
    I trudged in syndicated shoots;

continued

And that unlucky day when I
　Fired by mistake into the ground
Under a Lionel Edwards sky
　And felt disapprobation round.

The slow drive home by motor-car,
　A heavy Rover Landaulette,
Through Welwyn, Hatfield, Potters Bar,
　Tweed and cigar smoke, gloom and wet:

'How many times must I explain
　The way a boy should hold a gun?'
I recollect my father's pain
　At such a milksop for a son.

And now I see these fields once more
　Clothed, thank the Lord, in summer green,
Pale corn waves rippling to a shore
　The shadowy cliffs of elm between,

Colour-washed cottages reed-thatched
　And weather-boarded water mills,
Flint churches, brick and plaster patched,
　On mildly undistinguished hills –

They still are there. But now the shire
　Suffers a devastating change,
Its gentle landscape strung with wire,
　Old places looking ill and strange.

One can't be sure where London ends,
　New towns have filled the fields of root
Where father and his business friends
　Drove in the Landaulette to shoot;

Tall concrete standards line the lane,
　Brick boxes glitter in the sun:
Far more would these have caused him pain
　Than my mishandling of a gun.

John Betjeman

The gamekeeper's dotage

When he was eighty-two they opened
the first of the Supermarkets
on the main road. I don't think
he even noticed the mighty pyramids
of tins and washing-up liquid
at cut prices piled in the window –
although one Sunday morning
he caught in bare hands
the panful of boiling peas
that tipped from his black hob.
The house was silent and dirty;
it stank as if death were there already;
you couldn't be sure in rooms
where you peered as though through water
that hadn't been changed for years.
Of course, you never stayed long, (the stench,
the dinginess, the look that showed –
again - he didn't know who you were)
but let him for his pride's sake brew
a pot of tea, and mumble for awhile
among his towering memories, which,
towards the end came down to one.

It was troubling to visit him by then;
to step from the main road's redevelopment,
the loaded shopping-bags, the lines
of shining cars, into that hush
where over and over he lifted arms
like trembling sticks, pulled the trigger,
and killed it for the Duke - the last
stag on the great estate
that has been a public park for fifty years.

Tony Connor

An Arundel tomb

Side by side, their faces blurred,
The earl and countess lie in stone,
Their proper habits vaguely shown
As jointed armour, stiffened pleat,
And that faint hint of the absurd –
The little dogs under their feet.

Such plainness of the pre-baroque
Hardly involves the eye, until
It meets his left-hand gauntlet, still
Clasped empty in the other; and
One sees, with a sharp tender shock,
His hand withdrawn, holding her hand.

They would not think to lie so long.
Such faithfulness in effigy
Was just a detail friends would see:
A sculptor's sweet commissioned grace
Thrown off in helping to prolong
The Latin names around the base.

They would not guess how early in
Their supine stationary voyage
The air would change to soundless damage,
Turn the old tenantry away;
How soon succeeding eyes begin
To look, not read. Rigidly they

Persisted, linked, through lengths and breadths
Of time. Snow fell, undated. Light
Each summer thronged the glass. A bright
Litter of birdcalls strewed the same
Bone-riddled ground. And up the paths
The endless altered people came,

Washing at their identity.
Now, helpless in the hollow of
An unarmorial age, a trough
Of smoke in slow suspended skeins
Above their scrap of history
Only an attitude remains:

Time has transfigured them into
Untruth. The stone fidelity
They hardly meant has come to be
Their final blazon, and to prove
Our almost-instinct almost true:
What will survive of us is love.

Philip Larkin

Coral

This coral's shape echoes the hand
It hollowed. Its

Immediate absence is heavy. As pumice,
As your breast in my cupped palm.

Sea-cold, its nipple rasps like sand,
Its pores, like yours, shone with salt sweat.

Bodies in absence displace their weight,
And your smooth body, like none other

Creates an exact absence like this stone
Set on a table with a whitening wrack

Of souvenirs. It dares my hand
To claim what lovers' hands have never known:

The nature of the body of another.

Derek Walcott

Three baroque meditations

1

Do words make up the majesty
Of man, and his justice
Between the stones and the void?

How they watch us, the demons
Plugging their dumb wounds! When
Exorcized they shrivel yet thrive.

An owl plunges to its tryst
With a field-mouse in the sharp night.
My fire squeals and lies still.

Minerva, receive this hard
Praise: I speak well of Death;
I confess to the priest in me;

I am shadowed by the wise bird
Of necessity, the lithe
Paradigm Sleep-and-Kill.

2

Anguish bloated by the replete scream.
Flesh of abnegation: the poem
Moves grudgingly to its extreme form,

Vulnerable, to the lamp's fierce head
Of well-trimmed light. In darkness outside,
Foxes and rain-sleeked stones and the dead –

Aliens of such a theme – endure
Until I could cry 'Death! Death!' as though
To exacerbate that suave power;

But refrain. For I am circumspect,
Lifting the spicy lid of my tact
To sniff at the myrrh. It is perfect

In its impalpable bitterness,
Scent of a further country where worse
Furies promenade and bask their claws.

3 *The dead bride*

So white I was, he would have me cry
   'Unclean!' murderously
To heal me with far-fetched blood.

I writhed to conceive of him.
I clawed to becalm him.
Some nights, I witnessed his face in sleep

And dreamed of my father's
House. (By day he professed languages –
   Disciplines of languages) –

By day I cleansed my pink tongue
From its nightly prowl, its vixen-skill,
   His sacramental mouth

   That justified my flesh
And moved well among women
In nuances and imperatives.

This was the poet of a people's
   Love. I hated him. He weeps,
Solemnizing his loss.

Geoffrey Hill

111

Mrs Blow and her animals

There was a dog called Clanworthy
Who lived with his friend the cat Hopdance
In the house of Mrs Blow, a widow,
Upon a glade in Cluny.

Hey, Hopdance,
How is Mrs Blow?
So-so, said Hopdance,
Bow, said the dog.

Mrs Blow
Loved her animals very much
She often said:
I do not know what I should do
Without Hopdance and
Clanworthy.

They loved her too.

Hey, Hopdance,
How is Mrs Blow?
So-so, said Hopdance,
She is not very well, said the dog.

Hopdance fetched her a fish
Which she cooked by the fire.
That will do her good,
Said Hopdance; but, said the dog,
She must have wine as well as food.

Clanworthy, brave Clanworthy,
Clanworthy for aye
Through fire and water brought wine
That Mrs Blow might not die.

Mrs Blow has now become their only thought
And care,
All the other animals

In the forest of Cluny
Say there is no talking to them now
Because their only thought is Mrs Blow.
Hey Hopdance,
How is Mrs Blow?
Oh, very well now.
She is quite recovered, said the dog.

But a woodcutter has opined
It was the spirit of Mrs Blow he saw dancing one night
When a full moon fell on the glade of Cluny
With her animals, and that
Clanworthy and Hopdance
Stood upright upon their hind legs
Holding the hand of Mrs Blow the widow
As if she was a child.
If it was Mrs Blow
But he said he thought it was the ghost
Of Mrs Blow, her spirit; and that
The animals, too, did not look like animals; he said
It was three spirits playing ring-a-ring
With crowns on their head.

So everyone remembered then
That a long time ago
The King and Queen had lost their little children
As
A great witch had changed the boys into animals
And the girl into Mrs Blow the widow

Crying: Hopdance, go Hopdance; Clanworthy go,
For a hundred and seven years
Be the animals of Mrs Blow.

Everyone was glad it had come right
And that the princes and princess
Were dancing in the night.

Stevie Smith

Mandrakes

look for us among those
shy flowers opening
at night only
                in the
shadow, in the held breath
under oak trees listen for

rootshuffle or is it wind
    you won't find us, we
got small a long time back
we withdrew like the Picts
into fireside tale and rumour

we were terrible in our time
gaunt plants fertilized
by the leachings of hanged men
    knobby frames shrieking and
stumping around the planet

smaller and bushier now
prudent green men moving
in oakshadow or among reed
guardians of the young snake
                rearing from the water
                with the head and curving
                neck of a small dinosaur

we can outwait you for
ever if we need, lounging
leafy arms linked along
some park's path, damp fallen leaves
covering our itch to move

mouths open to the wind
sigh entering the sough
from the distant branches

like a rumour at your fireside

Thom Gunn

Address to the beasts

For us who, from the moment
we first are worlded,
lapse into disarray,

who seldom know exactly
what we are up to,
and, as a rule, don't want to,

what a joy to know,
even when we can't see or hear you,
that you are around,

though very few of you
find us worth looking at,
unless we come too close.

To you all scents are sacred
except our smell and those
we manufacture.

How promptly and ably
you execute Nature's policies,
and are never

lured into misconduct
except by some unlucky
chance imprinting.

Endowed from birth with good manners,
you wag no snobbish elbows,
don't leer,

don't look down your nostrils,
nor poke them into another
creature's business.

continued

Your own habitations
are cosy and private, not
pretentious temples.

Of course, you have to take lives
to keep your own, but never
kill for applause.

Compared with even your greediest,
how Non-U
our hunting gentry seem.

Exempt from taxation,
you have never felt the need
to become literate,

but your oral cultures
have inspired our poets to pen
dulcet verses,

and, though unconscious of God,
your Sung Eucharists are
more hallowed than ours.

Instinct is commonly said
to rule you: I would call it
Common Sense.

If you cannot engender
a genius like Mozart,
neither can you

plague the earth
with brilliant sillies like Hegel
or clever nasties like Hobbes.

Shall we ever become adulted,
as you all soon do?
It seems unlikely.

Indeed, one balmy day,
we might well become,
not fossils, but vapour.

Distinct now,
in the end we shall join you
(how soon all corpses look alike),

but you exhibit no signs
of knowing that you are sentenced.
Now, could that be why

we upstarts are often
jealous of your innocence,
but never envious?

W.H. Auden

On being asked to write a school hymn

Tune: Buckland
('Loving Shepherd of Thy Sheep')

On a starless night and still
Underneath a sleeping hill
Comes the cry of sheep and kine
From the slaughter house to mine.

Fearful is the call and near
That I do not want to hear,
Though it has been said by some
That the animal is dumb.

Gone the byre and gone the breeze
And the gently moving trees
As with stabbing eye they run
In a clear, electric sun.

continued

Now, red-fingered to their trade
With the shot and with the blade,
Rubber-booted angels white
Enter as the morning light.

But who wields that knife and gun
Does not strike the blow alone,
And there is no place to stand
Other than at his right hand.

God, who does not dwell on high
In the wide, unwinking sky,
And whose quiet counsels start
Simply from the human heart,

Teach us strong and teach us true
What to say and what to do,
That we love as best we can
All Thy creatures. Even man.

Amen.

Charles Causley

118

To be called a bear

Bears gash the forest trees
  To mark the bounds
  Of their own hunting grounds;
They follow the wild bees
  Point by point home
  For love of honeycomb;
They browse on blueberries.

Then should I stare
If I am called a bear,
And is it not the truth?
Unkempt and surly with a sweet tooth
I tilt my muzzle toward the starry hub
Where Queen Callisto guards her cub;

But envy those that here
  All winter breathing slow
  Sleep warm under the snow,
That yawn awake when the skies clear,
  And lank with longing grow
No more than one brief month a year.

Robert Graves

Au Jardin des Plantes

The gorilla lay on his back,
One hand cupped under his head,
Like a man.

Like a labouring man tired with work,
A strong man with his strength burnt away
In the toil of earning a living.

continued

119

Only of course he was not tired out with work,
Merely with boredom; his terrible strength
All burnt away by prodigal idleness.

A thousand days, and then a thousand days,
Idleness licked away his beautiful strength,
He having no need to earn a living.

It was all laid on, free of charge.
We maintained him, not for doing anything,
But for being what he was.

And so that Sunday morning he lay on his back,
Like a man, like a worn-out man,
One hand cupped under his terrible hard head.

Like a man, like a man,
One of those we maintain, not for doing anything,
But for being what they are.

A thousand days, and then a thousand days,
With everything laid on, free of charge,
They cup their heads in prodigal idleness.

John Wain

Talking to mice

Plural the verdicts we cast on the creatures we have to
    shake hands with:
*Creepy! Get HER! Good Lord, what an oddity! One to steer
    clear of!*
Fun! Impossible! Nice, but a bore! An adorable monster!
But those animates which we call in our arrogance *dumb* are
judged as a species and classed by the melodramatic
    division,

either *Goodies* or *Baddies*. So spiders and roaches and flies we

excommunicate as - ugh! - all irredeemably evil,

Dreck to be stamped on or swatted, abolished without any hover.

Mice, *per contra*, except to a few hysterical women,

rank among the most comely of all the miniature mammals

who impinge on our lives, for our smell doesn't seem to alarm them,

visitors whom we can jump with, co-agents it doesn't seem phoney

we should endow with a *You*, as from now on I shall in these verses,

though my grammatical shift will be out of your ken for, alas, you

never have managed, as all successful parasites must, to

crack the code of your host, wise up on what habits can travel.

Ah! if only you had, with what patience we would have trained you

how to obtemper your greeds, recalling the way that our Nannies

moulded our nursery *mœurs*, bechiding whenever we turned our

noses up at a dish - *Now remember the starving Armenians!* -

and when we gobbled—*Enough! Leave something for nice Mr Manners!* -

cited you suitable maxims. *Good Little Mice never gnaw through*

wood-work or nibble at packages. Good Little Mice never scatter

droppings that have to be swept up. Good Little Mice get a tid-bit,

Bad Little Mice die young. Then, adapting an adage of lovers,

Two Little Mice are a company. Three Little Mice are a rabble.

continued

All through the Spring and the Summer, while you were still
   only a couple,
fit-sides we dwelt in a peace as idyllic as only a Beatrix
Potter could paint. In September, though, this was
   abrupted: you must have
littered for, lo! quite suddenly, there were a swarm of you,
   messing
everything up until no cache was aloof to your insults.
What occurred now confirmed that ancient political axiom:
When Words fail to persuade, then Physical Force gives the
   orders.
Knowing you trusted in us, and would never believe an
   unusual
object pertaining to men could be there for a sinister
   purpose,
traps were baited and one by one you were fatally
   humbugged.
All fourteen of you perished. To move from where we'd been
   sipping
cocktails and giving ear, translated out of ourselves, to
Biedermeyer Duets or Strauss in *Metamorphosen*
mourning the end of his world, and enter the kitchen to find
   there
one more broken cadaver, its black eyes beadily staring,
obumbrated a week. We had felt no talent to murder,
it was against our pluck. Why, why then? For *raisons*
   d'État. As
householders we had behaved exactly as every State does,
when there is something it wants, and a minor one gets in
   the way.

W.H. Auden

Tinkers

Three princes rigged like scarecrows
Straggled along the shore
And every clucking wife
Ran in and barred her door.

Their coats hung in such shreds
The dogs barked as they came.
O but their steps were a dance,
Their eyes all black flame!

The wife's undone her pack
And spread it at our door.
Grails, emeralds, peacock feathers
Scattered over the floor.

The man flashed his bow,
His fiddle had only one string,
But where is the sun-drowned lark
Like that can sing?

The dark boy wore his rags
Like an April-wakened tree,
Or as a drift of seaweed
Glitters on the arms of the sea.

Princes, they ruled in our street
A long shining age,
While Merran peeped through her curtains
Like a hawk from a cage.

Paupers, they filthied our pier
A piece of one afternoon,
Then scowled, stank, shouldered their packs
And cursed and were gone.

George Mackay Brown

The O-filler

One noon in the library, I watched a man –
imagine! – filling in O's, a little, rumpled
nobody of a man, who licked his stub of pencil
and leaned over every O with a loving care,
shading it neatly, exactly to its edges
until the open pages
were pocked and dotted with solid O's, like towns
and capitals on a map. And yet, so peppered,
the book appeared inhabited and complete.

That whole afternoon, as the light outside softened
and the library groaned woodenly,
he worked and worked, his o-so-patient shading
descending like an eyelid over each open O
for page after page. Not once did he miss one,
or hover even a moment over an *a*
or an *e* or a *p* or a *g*. Only the O's –
oodles of O's, O's multitudinous, O's manifold,
O's italic and roman.
And what light on his crumpled face when he discovered –
as I supposed – odd words like *zoo* and *ooze*,
  polo, oolong and *odontology*!

Think now. In that limitless library,
all round the steep-shelved walls, bulging in their bindings,
books stood, waiting. Heaven knows how many
he had so far filled, but still there remained
uncountable volumes of O-laden prose, and odes
with inflated capital O's (in the manner of Shelley),
O-bearing Bibles and biographies,
even whole sections devoted to O alone,
all his for the filling. Glory, glory, glory!

How utterly open and endless the world must have seemed
    to him,
how round and ample! Think of it. A pencil
was all he needed. Life was one wide O.

And why, at the end of things, should O's not be closed
as eyes are? I envied him, for in my place
across the table from him, had I accomplished
anything as firm as he had, or as fruitful?
What could I show? A handful of scrawled lines,
an afternoon yawned and wondered away,
and a growing realisation that in time
even my scribbled words would come
under his grubby thumb, and the blinds be drawn
on all my O's, with only this thought for comfort -
that when he comes to this poem, a proper joy
may amaze his wizened face and, o, a pure pleasure
make his meticulous pencil quiver.

Alastair Reid

The piano tuner

Every six months his white stick brings him,
Punctilious to the minim stroke of nine
On the day we dread. Edgy at his knock,
We infuse a grudging warmth into voices
Asking his health, attempt to ease his coat
From him, which courtesy he refuses;

And usher him to the instrument. He entrusts
Us with nothing, disdains from his black tent,
Our extended hands where the awkward staircase
Bends, rattles the banisters with his bag,
Crabs past the chairs. Finally at the keyboard
He discharges quick arpeggios of judgment.

'As I expected,' he says, dismissing us;
And before we close the door excludes us
Further, intent in his flummox of strange tools
And a language beyond us. He begins to adjust
And insist on the quotients and ratios
Of order in encased reverberant wire.

All morning, then, downstairs we cower;
The thin thunder of decibels, octaves slowly
Made absolute, which will not break into storm,
Dividing us from him. The house is not the same
Until long after he leaves, having made one thing
Perfect. 'Now play,' say his starched eyes.

John Ormond

The explosion

On the day of the explosion
Shadows pointed towards the pithead:
In the sun the slagheap slept.

Down the lane came men in pitboots
Coughing oath-edged talk and pipe-smoke,
Shouldering off the freshened silence.

One chased after rabbits; lost them;
Came back with a nest of lark's eggs;
Showed them; lodged them in the grasses.

So they passed in beards and moleskins,
Fathers, brothers, nicknames, laughter,
Through the tall gates standing open.

At noon, there came a tremor; cows
Stopped chewing for a second; sun,
Scarfed as in a heat-haze, dimmed.

The dead go on before us, they
Are sitting in God's house in comfort,
We shall see them face to face -

Plain as lettering in the chapels
It was said, and for a second
Wives saw men of the explosion

Larger than in life they managed -
Gold as on a coin, or walking
Somehow from the sun towards them,

One showing the eggs unbroken.

Philip Larkin

The Don Brown Route

Over your head the climbing blue
Sky observes your lonely foot.
Through the lens of language I
Focus on the Don Brown Route.

From where I am, even if I shout,
You will not hear. You climb in slow
Motion on silence on the face
Full of happy, full of woe.

Today is very nothing like
Any other day that once soared
In this place. My lens suddenly
Is crossed with the black of a near bird.

Today is almost without winds
And I can see your fingers brush
Your next hold clean and the sand drift
Fine like the smoke of your own ash.

Through the lens of language each
Act hangs for a long time.
Floated out in the iodine air
Your motion comes to me like home

Ing birds meaning to say something
I should be able to read. Reach
For the hold three feet above your pressing
Cheek bright at the edge of your stretch.

Set your Northern toe-cap in
To where your own weather has set
A ledge of spar like an offered journey
Across the cobbles of your street.

At least I am not putting you off
Through the dumb lens I see you through.
I can't nudge your climbing foot
Or shout out to you what to do.

Yet do not lean too far in
To the father face or it will
Astonish you with a granite kiss
And send you packing over the sill.

If you fall, remember no one will see
You tumbling lonely down. Only
I through this bad focus will see.
Why do you imagine Gravity lonely?

And over your head the climbing blue
Sky observes your lonely foot.
Stopped in the lens of language you
Slowly establish the Don Brown Route.

W.S. Graham

A constable calls

His bicycle stood at the window-sill,
The rubber cowl of a mud-splasher
Skirting the front mudguard,
Its fat black handlegrips

Heating in the sunlight, the 'spud'
Of the dynamo gleaming and cocked back,
The pedal treads hanging relieved
Of the boot of the law.

continued

His cap was upside down
On the floor, next his chair.
The line of its pressure ran like a bevel
In his slightly sweating hair.

He had unstrapped
The heavy ledger, and my father
Was making tillage returns
In acres, roods, and perches.

Arithmetic and fear
I sat staring at the polished holster
With its buttoned flap, the braid cord
Looped into the revolver butt.

'Any other root crops?
Mangolds? Marrowstems? Anything like that?'
'No.' But was there not a line
Of turnips where the seed ran out

In the potato field? I assumed
Small guilts and sat
Imagining the black hole in the barracks.
He stood up, shifted the baton-case

Further round on his belt,
Closed the domesday book,
Fitted his cap back with two hands,
And looked at me as he said goodbye.

A shadow bobbed in the window.
He was snapping the carrier spring
Over the ledger. His boot pushed off
And the bicycle ticked, ticked, ticked.

Seamus Heaney

The laundress

Her chair drawn to the door,
A basket at her feet,
She sat against the sun
And stitched a linen sheet.
Over harrowed Flanders
August moved the wheat.

Poplars sharing the wind
With Saxony and France
Dreamed at her gate,
Soared in a Summer trance.
A cluck in the cobbled yard:
A shadow changed its stance.

As a fish disturbs the pond
And sinks without a stain
The heels of ripeness fluttered
Under her apron. Then
Her heart grew strained and light
As the shell that shields the grain.

Bluntly through the doorway
She stared at shed and farm,
At yellow fields unstitching
About the hoarded germ,
At land that would spread white
When she had reached her term.

The sower plumps his acre,
Flanders turns to the heat,
The winds of Heaven winnow
And the wheels grind the wheat.
She searched in her basket
And fixed her ruffled sheet.

Thomas Kinsella

At his father's grave

Here lies a shoe-maker whose knife and hammer
Fell idle at the height of summer,
Who was not missed so much as when the rain
Of winter brought him back to mind again.

He was no preacher but his working text
Was *See all dry this winter and the next.*
Stand still. Remember his two hands, his laugh,
His craftsmanship. They are his epitaph.

John Ormond

My father, dying

At summer's succulent end,
the house is green-stained.
I reach for my father's hand

and study his ancient nails.
Feeble-bodied, yet at intervals
a sweetness appears and prevails.

The heavy-scented night
seems to get at his throat.
It is as if the dark coughed.

In the other rooms of the house,
the furniture stands mumchance.
Age has engraved his face.

Cradling his wagged-out-chin,
I shave him, feeling bone
stretching the waxed skin.

By his bed, the newspaper lies furled.
He has grown too old
to unfold the world,

which has dwindled to the size of a sheet.
His room has a stillness to it.
I do not call it waiting, but I wait,

anxious in the dark, to see if
the butterfly of his breath
has fluttered clear of death.

There is so much might be said,
dear old man, before I find you dead;
but we have become too separate

now in human time
to unravel all the interim
as your memory goes numb.

But there is no need for you to tell –
no words, no wise counsel,
no talk of dying well.

We have become mostly hands
and voices in your understanding.
The whole household is pending.

I am not ready
to be without your frail and wasted body,
your miscellaneous mind-way,

the faltering vein of your life.
Each evening, I am loth
to leave you to your death.

Nor will I dwell on
the endless, cumulative question
I ask, being your son.

continued

But on any one
of these nights soon,
for you, the dark will not crack with dawn,

and then I will begin
with you that hesitant conversation
going on and on and on.

Alastair Reid

The journey

Mother, hear the wind keening over the Goss Moor,
Tregeagle's sighs, emptying the bottomless Dozmare
Pool. Seeing the world again begins to bore
You. You rub seized joints. I ask you how you are
And the wind fails to force the car
Off the A30. Yes, it is good of me to drive so far,

For one almost as old and bald as Dozmare,
Her life, apart from me, featureless as Goss Moor.
I compute how far
We have to go: seven hours. She who bore
Me is pressed, small, while the decimal nines are
Flickering into noughts, back into the car,

As I was, waiting. I ask how you are;
Must I wind down the window a shade, raise the car-
Heater? It is wrinkled Tregeagle emptying the Dozmare
Pool in you, discomfort, pain, that never fall far
Before rising to the same level. Your harpings bore
Me like this incessant wind over the Goss Moor.

And I cannot look sideways in the car,
It is too painful to see how shrunken you are,
Tacitly, since last the Goss Moor
Shot past us, and hidden Dozmare;
Three thousand miles on the gauge since I came so far
To fetch you. That January day you bore

Me, did the journey feel so far?
Image of starry countdowns that move and bore
Us, I dice with the petrol countdown, see if the car
Will reach the next pump, past Bodmin Moor.
You rest trustful in my omniscience. Old Dozmare
Mother, what strange things and what strangers we are.

I know these three weeks you will bore
Me. I don't read your letters when you are far
Away, those cheerful comforting lies. So; till you are
Dead, as something wants, and, dead, I drive this car
Or the next, for the last time up through the moor
That rose when Dozmare was sea, and sees the end of
    Dozmare.

I help you struggle from the car, to a moorstone. You bore
Your own small Dozmare in thin soil. For we are water and
    moor,
And far journeyers together. Whatever else we are.

D.M. Thomas

Reference back

That was a pretty one, I heard you call
From the unsatisfactory hall
To the unsatisfactory room where I
Played record after record, idly,
Wasting my time at home, that you
Looked so much forward to.

Oliver's *Riverside Blues*, it was. And now
I shall, I suppose, always remember how
The flock of notes those antique negroes blew
Out of Chicago air into
A huge remembering pre-electric horn
The year after I was born
Three decades later made this sudden bridge
From your unsatisfactory age
To my unsatisfactory prime.

Truly, though our element is time,
We are not suited to the long perspectives
Open at each instant of our lives.
They link us to our losses: worse,
They show us what we have as it once was,
Blindingly undiminished, just as though
By acting differently we could have kept it so.

Philip Larkin

Mother of the groom

What she remembers
Is his glistening back
In the bath, his small boots
In the ring of boots at her feet.

Hands in her voided lap,
She hears a daughter welcomed.
It's as if he kicked when lifted
And slipped her soapy hold.

Once soap would ease off
The wedding ring
That's bedded forever now
In her clapping hand.

Seamus Heaney

Walking away
for Sean

It is eighteen years ago, almost to the day -
A sunny day with the leaves just turning,
The touch-lines new-ruled - since I watched you play
Your first game of football, then, like a satellite
Wrenched from its orbit, go drifting away

Behind a scatter of boys. I can see
You walking away from me towards the school
With the pathos of a half-fledged thing set free
Into a wilderness, the gait of one
Who finds no path where the path should be.

continued

That hesitant figure, eddying away
Like a winged seed loosened from its parent stem,
Has something I never quite grasp to convey
About nature's give-and-take - the small, the scorching
Ordeals which fire one's irresolute clay.

I have had worse partings, but none that so
Gnaws at my mind still. Perhaps it is roughly
Saying what God alone could perfectly show -
How selfhood begins with a walking away,
And love is proved in the letting go.

C. Day Lewis

Maiden name

Marrying left your maiden name disused.
Its five light sounds no longer mean your face,
Your voice, and all your variants of grace;
For since you were so thankfully confused
By law with someone else, you cannot be
Semantically the same as that young beauty:
It was of her that these two words were used.

Now it's a phrase applicable to no one,
Lying just where you left it, scattered through
Old lists, old programmes, a school prize or two,
Packets of letters tied with tartan ribbon -
Then is it scentless, weightless, strengthless, wholly
Untruthful? Try whispering it slowly.
No, it means you. Or, since you're past and gone,

It means what we feel now about you then:
How beautiful you were, and near, and young,
So vivid, you might still be there among
Those first few days, unfingermarked again.
So your old name shelters our faithfulness,
Instead of losing shape and meaning less
With your depreciating luggage laden.

Philip Larkin

Juliet and her nurse

Under the hot slanting Italian sun,
two woman-shapes.

This one casting a lean upright shadow:
that one casting a soft rounded shadow.

Here, all quickness, insistence:
there, a habit of circling.

And why should she not circle?
She ranges for nourishment far distant.

Her landscape lies spread beneath the crags
where she sits memoried, brooding: she sails out
on broad dusty wings now and then,
to look it over.

And why should she not be insistent?
(She, she: haec, illa: our tongue does not say it.)
Needs newly awakened are needles.
One night in his arms is a down payment:
the rest is to come soon, it must come, it must.

They are like water:
this one leaping from the rock, unwarmed, unstained,
exclaiming in diamond spray, avid for contact,
contact with stone, wood, air, clay, skin,
with the throats of animals and men:

that one broadened out, standing,
in places very deep, calm on the surface,
in places shaded by old trees.

The young woman is hungry.
She wants love, which is to say she wants suffering,
joy, fury, repletion and forgiveness.
She wants to throw herself over the steep rocks.

continued

The old woman is satisfied:
her body moves slowly and needs little,
stored with the rich protein of her memories.

Memories of when she, too,
cast a lean upright shadow:
when she threw herself over the steep rocks
and he was standing below, eager, and caught her.

The young woman will not be caught.
Down the rock-face dashes the clear water
unwarmed, unstained, wasted:
no old trees will shade her,
there will be no quiet depths.
We know the story.

John Wain

Children, beggars and schoolteachers

Careless of the future, tolerant of today,
Gay in their frozen moment, and so warm:
Flat feet buffet the pavement:
                    things fear them,
They have no fear. And these are children,
For whom, they say, all is intimidating, mysterious,
                    unknown.

Bent in ugly balls against the wall,
The past forgotten, a dim and distant present,
                    the reckoned future unresented:
Only a stump of arm, a withered leg -
                    that is
Their sedentary occupation. The quiet beggars
Sleeping with their hands held out.
All mysteries solved for them, no possible fears.

In nervous transit from tram to tram,
A present past, a dubious present, and a future
                      full of fears.
Feet that mistrust the slithering earth: we,
The teachers, bearers of diplomas
                        and mysteries still unsolved,
We who should guide the children,
                  lest they
Should later come to begging.

D.J. Enright

Who?

Who is that child I see wandering, wandering
Down by the side of the quivering stream?
Why does he seem not to hear, though I call to him?
Where does he come from, and what is his name?

Why do I see him at sunrise and sunset
Taking, in old-fashioned clothes, the same track?
Why, when he walks, does he cast not a shadow
Though the sun rises and falls at his back?

Why does the dust lie so thick on the hedgerow
By the great field where a horse pulls the plough?
Why do I see only meadows, where houses
Stand in a line by the riverside now?

Why does he move like a wraith by the water,
Soft as the thistledown on the breeze blown?
When I draw near him so that I may hear him,
Why does he say that his name is my own?

Charles Causley

Bleeding a stone is walking by the sea

I move in memory as the fish in water
Sings happy in its silences, and cry
Heavy the ocean covers us up later
But we shall break the rock before we die.
That rock is riven where a bright spectre shakes
Her mushroom head to warn us away,
As here, to tell the proud star that it breaks
Bleeding a stone is walking by the sea.

So rusted the chained sailor in his berth
When the wave took him hissing in the night;
Not knowing love or death he would not die,
But stopped his skeleton as it stepped forth.
So I look inward to the birth of love
And see, trapped in the mazes of the skull,
That winged authority of life who cries:
Bleeding a stone is walking by the sea.

Out of a seventh wave the first germ sprang
Into the manger of my arms, and spoke:
'I am the word that the affirming tongue
Began a world with. All living things evoke
The law of love that suspends and sustains
Each in all others, as I lie singing here.
The crime is married nightly to the pain,
Bleeding a stone is walking by the sea.'

That little boat is loaded with a catch
Of all creation, and the descending star
Drops slowly and for ever through a loving
Eye. The liar, the lamb and the lion are
Perpetually caught up in that great embrace
Uniting all that will be, is, and was.
And where old Adam once sinned on a shore
Bleeding a stone is walking by the sea.

O who has spun the worst world on its cold
Circle of lessening ignorance and love
Into such darkness? Enormity so old
That now the pride that stood a fish upright
Crushes us down to ashes. Reprove, reprove
You angel authority from whom we have
The liberty to love, reprove, reprove, and save!
Bleeding a stone is walking by the grave.

George Barker

Missing the sea

Something removed roars in the ears of this house,
Hangs its drapes windless, stuns mirrors
Till reflections lack substance.

Some sound like the gnashing of windmills ground
To a dead halt;
A deafening absence, a blow.

It hoops this valley, weighs this mountain,
Estranges gesture, pushes this pencil
Through a thick nothing now,

Freights cupboards with silence, folds sour laundry
Like the clothes of the dead left exactly
As the dead behaved by the beloved,

Incredulous, expecting occupancy.

Derek Walcott

Thank you, fog

Grown used to New York weather,
all too familiar with Smog,
You, Her unsullied Sister,
I'd quite forgotten and what
You bring to British winters:
now native knowledge returns.

Sworn foe to festination,
daunter of drivers and planes,
volants, of course, will curse You,
but how delighted I am
that You've been lured to visit
Wiltshire's witching countryside
for a whole week at Christmas,
that no one can scurry where
my cosmos is contracted
to an ancient manor-house
and four Selves, joined in friendship,
Jimmy, Tania, Sonia, Me.

Outdoors a shapeless silence,
for even those birds whose blood
is brisk enough to bid them
abide here all the year round,
like the merle and the mavis,
at Your cajoling refrain
their jocund interjections,
no cock considers a scream,
vaguely visible, tree-tops
rustle not but stay there, so
efficiently condensing
Your damp to definite drops.

Indoors specific spaces,
cosy, accommodate to
reminiscence and reading,
crosswords, affinities, fun:
refected by a sapid
supper and regaled by wine,
we sit in a glad circle,
each unaware of our own
nose but alert to the others,
making the most of it, for
how soon we must re-enter,
when lenient days are done,
the world of work and money
and minding our p's and q's.

No summer sun will ever
dismantle the global gloom
cast by the Daily Papers,
vomiting in slip-shod prose
the facts of filth and violence
that we're too dumb to prevent:
our earth's a sorry spot, but
for this special interim,
so restful yet so festive,
Thank You, Thank You, Thank You, Fog.

W.H. Auden

Notes on the poets and poems

Dannie Abse, b. Cardiff, 1923. Educated at the University of Wales, King's College London, and Westminster Hospital. Abse is a physician (MRCS, LRCP) with a London practice. He has written many plays and three novels as well as a large body of verse.

W.H. Auden, b. York 1907. Educated at Gresham's School, Holt, and Oxford. Many jobs as schoolmaster and university lecturer; Professor of Poetry, Oxford University, 1956-61; much free-lance work. Took American nationality in 1938, but from the mid fifties spent much of his time in Europe; died in Oxford in 1973.

Always a magpie of unusual pieces of information, Auden enjoyed bringing rare and obsolete words into his poems; thus in the poems printed here we find 'obtemper' (to comply with, yield to, submit, obey, or transitively, to restrain), 'obumrate' (overshadow, shade, darken), 'osse' (signify - a fourteenth-century west midland word still sometimes heard in speech between the Welsh border and Cumberland, and perhaps a memory from Auden's childhood). 'Period' and 'worlded' are I suppose coinage of Auden's own; 'glop', presumably, means 'stare mindlessly'. Auden's word-games may not add much to his poems but neither do they take anything away, and personally I enjoy them.

'Moon landing' is full of the wit of the elder Auden, his deft use of literary and other allusions. Dr Johnson remarked of something that it was worth seeing, but 'not worth going to see'; Auden neatly inverts this in stanza 6 — the journey might be worth it but the sight isn't. Another characteristic of the later Auden is his ironic, yet compassionate, detachment; his search for solitude, his need to drop out of the parade. The young Auden had marched with the parade, frequently invoking 'history'; the elder Auden speaks of 'the usual squalid mess called history'.

'Thank you, fog': Auden lived for many years in New York; towards the end of his life he spent much more time in England, where 'native knowledge returned'. This poem is very English (even the form seems to be an adaptation of the Anglo-Saxon alliterative metre). One of the poets who have meant most to the English was the Roman poet Horace: Italian peasants in the eighteenth century vaguely supposed Horace to have been an Englishman because of the number of English who asked the way to his house; and Horace was the great poet of the private life, of the happiness to be found in laying down the cares of the world and living quietly and privately in the country. In our century of hurried long-distance travel, when people are always racing to stations and airports, a fog which immobolizes everything can be a true ally of the Horatian spirit; it helps the four friends in the poem to feel isolated from the world and cosy in their relationship.

George Barker, b. Essex 1913. Educated in London; has lived in America and Italy. A prolific poet, Barker has also written radio plays and novels.

The poem for Eliot's birthday reflects the strongly religious strain, without the underpinning of formal belief, which Barker shares with his near-contemporary Dylan Thomas. Eliot had a strong religious faith in an age of doctrinal uncertainty; the poet stands apart from this faith ('the visions whistle as they rot') but nevertheless feels that such belief can 'tame the great negations' if only by the strength of the individual who holds it: Eliot tames them 'with his name'.

John Betjeman, b. Highgate, London, 1906. Educated at Marlborough and Oxford. Much occasional literary criticism; books on architecture and topography; numerous volumes of verse since 1931. Knighted 1969. Poet Laureate since 1972.

George Mackay Brown, b. Stromness, Orkney, 1921. Educated locally, at Newbattle Abbey and at Edinburgh University. Born and bred in the Orkney Islands where he still lives. Convert to Roman Catholicism since 1961.

Charles Causley, b. Launceston, Cornwall, 1917. Educated locally. Royal Navy 1940-6. Was for many years a schoolmaster in Cornwall. Visiting Fellow in Poetry, University of Exeter, 1973-4. Queen's Medal for Poetry 1967.

147

Tony Connor, b. Manchester 1930. Left school at 14. National Service (driving a tank) 1948–50. Worked as a textile designer in Manchester for some fifteen years; since then posts at universities, mostly American. Lives in Middletown, Connecticut; regularly visits England.

Anthony Conran, b. Kharghpur, India, 1931. Educated at University College, Bangor, North Wales, where he has been a research fellow and tutor since 1957. Many volumes of verse; his main collection is *Spirit Level* (1974). Edited *Penguin Book of Welsh Verse* 1967.

Lawrence Durrell, b. Julundur, India, 1912. Educated at Darjeeling and Canterbury. Many jobs; has lived mostly abroad, in south-eastern Europe and, since 1957, in France. Many volumes of verse and prose; much topographical writing.

D.J. Enright, b. Warwickshire 1920; educated locally and at Cambridge. Spent many years as a university teacher of English literature in foreign countries (Egypt, Japan, Germany, Thailand, Singapore), now works with a firm of London publishers. Was co-editor for two years of the magazine *Encounter.* Poet, novelist, critic, hard-hitting controversialist, Enright is a formidable presence on the English (or any) scene.

W.S. Graham, b. Greenock, Scotland, 1918. Educated locally and at Newbattle Abbey. Has been lecturer at New York University; mainly free-lance.

'The Don Brown Route' is an excellent example of poetry in double perspective: it is equally 'about' the rock-climber going up a face and the poet writing a poem about it. In literal terms, at the moment the poem shows us, the poet is not actually writing but watching the climber through binoculars, with that uncanny sense they give one of being close to the observed scene while actually being too remote to make any difference to it ('At least I am not putting you off'). The perfectly observed detail brings the climber very near to us, the readers: on a windless day, the sand he brushes off drifts down like his own ash (cremation ash, presumably; he is close to death all the time he is climbing, and he is not going up with a cigarette in his mouth). But because of the poet's habit of mind, the lens through which he is seeing the climber is the lens of language: to write about anything is a way of fixing it – in the lens of language 'each Act hangs for a long time'; also to bring out its inner significance – each movement of the climber is to the poet a signal, brought by a homing bird (our perceptions are like pigeons that fly in with messages) that he 'should be able to read'. Like the poems by MacNeice (p. 24) and D.M. Thomas (p. 27) this is a statement about writing poetry – though not *only* that. It is also about landscape and region; because Don Brown is a Northerner, the geological pressures that split the rock into a ledge by which he can climb up were part of his identity, 'your own weather'.

Robert Graves, b. London 1895. Educated at Charterhouse and Oxford. Served in the trenches in the First World War. Settled in Deyà, Majorca, in 1929; has lived there ever since with interruptions for the Spanish Civil War and the Second World War. Clark Lecturer, Cambridge, 1954; Professor of Poetry, Oxford, 1961-6. Numerous books of poetry, criticism, fiction; numerous prizes and awards; world-wide acclaim especially in the last thirty years.

Thom Gunn, b. Gravesend 1929. Educated at University College School, London, and Cambridge. National Service in the Army 1948-50. Taught at the University of California, Berkeley, 1958-66. Since then, free-lance writer. Lives in San Francisco.

The mandrake: this is a root-plant whose roots bear a grotesque resemblance to the human form; it is the mandragoras of the Ancient Greeks, and is mentioned in the Bible (Genesis 30: 14-17). It is credited with both sinister and innocent magical powers; but the problem was how to obtain it, because (tradition asserted) as it was pulled up it gave a scream that drove the hearer mad.

Michael Hamburger, b. Berlin 1924; emigrated to England 1933. Educated in Germany, Edinburgh, London, and finally

Oxford. Served in the Army 1943–7. Many academic posts; mainly free-lance. Numerous volumes of verse, original and translated, and of criticism; autobiography, *A Mug's Game*, 1973.

Seamus Heaney, b. County Derry 1939. Educated locally and at Queen's University, Belfast. Numerous awards; academic posts in Ireland and America.

John Heath-Stubbs, b. London 1918. Educated at Worcester College for the blind and Queen's College, Oxford. Has been schoolteacher, publisher; taught English literature in Egypt, in America and at home. Queen's Medal for Poetry 1973. In *Who's Who*, Mr Heath-Stubbs gives his recreation as 'taxonomy', which means the science of classification, or that part of any subject which is especially concerned with classifying. I think he is perfectly serious in this: he has an enormous knowledge of birds, animals, plants, rocks, mythology, theology, history, literature and music, and can always tell you to what order or sub-order anything belongs.

In 'To the mermaid at Zennor', 'the Jennifer' is a half-human creature known to folk-lore, and appearing in various stories and superstitions; the name is related to Guenevere, tragic heroine of the Arthurian cycle.

Geoffrey Hill, b. Bromsgrove, Worcestershire, 1932. Educated locally and at Oxford. Teaches at the University of Leeds.

In printing 'Three baroque meditations' I am breaking a self-imposed rule. Believing that it is unfair to commend to other people's attention poems I do not understand myself, I have generally printed no poem of which I would not feel able to give a prose paraphrase, however clumsy. The exceptions are these three poems of Hill's (the slighter, haunting 'Merlin' I think I do understand) and George Barker's 'Bleeding a stone is walking by the sea': poems that have a mysterious power to which I respond without 'understanding' them in the prose sense. (I could, of course concoct a paraphrase, but it would be guesswork.)

Ted Hughes, b. Mytholmroyd, Yorkshire, 1930. Educated locally and at Cambridge. National Service in RAF. Has worked as rose-gardener and night-watchman. Queen's Medal for Poetry 1974. Hughes is active as a dramatist as well as a poet, writing for television and radio as well as what used to be called 'closet-drama' - plays intended (or, at any rate, destined) to be read rather than performed.

Clive James, b. Sydney, Australia, 1939; came to England in 1962; studied at Cambridge, where he was President of the Footlights. Has always been involved in show business as lyric-writer, entertainer, critic; contributor to many papers; currently television critic of the *Observer*.

Elizabeth Jennings, b. Boston, Lincolnshire, 1926; soon moved to Oxford where her father was medical officer. Educated at Oxford, both school and university. Has worked in publishing and as a librarian; mainly free-lance.
   'Elegy on W. H. Auden' is strung on allusions to Auden's life and work. As a boy he was interested in mining, engineering and geology; in middle life bought a house in Kirchstetten, Austria, where he spent the summers; his last home was at Christ Church, Oxford. *The Orators* and *The Sea and the Mirror* are two of his large-scale works.

Thomas Kinsella, b. Dublin 1928. Educated at University College, Dublin. In Irish civil service 1948–65; since then, writer in residence and professor of English at various American universities.

Philip Larkin, b. Coventry, 1922. Educated locally and at Oxford. Librarian of the University of Hull since 1955. Queen's Medal for Poetry 1965. Has written two novels, and occasional literary criticism; feature writer on jazz for *Daily Telegraph* 1961–71. Edited *The New Oxford Book of Modern English Verse*, an important and controversial anthology, 1972.
   Larkin often uses very economical means to make important statements: 'Days', for instance, declares that the ultimate metaphysical questions are insoluble, the world's religions and

philosophies no safe guides; and all this is captured in the one dream-like image of the two men of conventional wisdom, in their formal and perhaps old-fashioned dress, 'running' in vain over the fields; the 'doctor' is I think a doctor of philosophy rather than of medicine. The first six lines of the poem obviously exist for the sake of the last four.

Larkin's work is intensely concerned with time and its effect on human lives; we live in time as fish live in water and birds live in air – it is 'our element' – yet we are so much less at ease in our element than they. In 'Reference back', as so often, Larkin makes his point through an ordinary, everyday situation. The poet is on a visit to his mother; she has been looking forward to his 'time at home', whereas he can think of nothing better to do than play old gramophone records. One of them is a piece of traditional jazz played by Joe ('King') Oliver and his band ('those antique negroes') on a precise date, 'the year after I was born', so that the poet himself looks back, to the time of his birth when his mother was young, then forward again to the present, his unsatisfactory prime and her unsatisfactory age, and perceives, for the ten-thousandth time, a 'sudden bridge'. Life often turns out disappointingly, and our memory and our sense of time 'link us to our losses' where a bird or fish would simply forget about them; we intensify this by inventing things like the gramophone, which even in its primitive, pre-electric phase was efficiently 'remembering'.

Peter Levi, b. Ruislip 1931. Educated at Beaumont College and Campion Hall Oxford. A classical scholar with an interest in archaeology, Levi has written a travel book about Afghanistan, *The Light Garden of the Angel King* (1972), and translated, with a commentary, the voluminous *Description of Greece* by Pausanias, a Greek writer of the early Christian era. Levi's *Collected Poems* came out in 1975.

'To poets in prison without trial': Levi is often a 'difficult' poet, not in the sense that his drift is hard to see, but that he works directly through images which he presents to the reader as images, without unpacking them into discourse. Understanding why the waste of the poets' lives is like 'solemn cries of ruined walls' is an emotional rather than intellectual matter, as all poetry will be to some extent. However, one can offer guidelines. Throughout history, and especially in our age of all-engulfing mass repressions, many poets have been imprisoned and murdered by the regime. In some cases we have heard of them and even read poems they wrote during their ordeal (we have, for instance, the unbearably moving poems written by the Hungarian poet Radnóty in a German concentration camp); but in far more cases the poets were just extinguished, and perhaps in some cases had not yet done the work that would have brought them recognition as poets at all. In such cases the poet's message is 'useless'; the beauty of his work, written or still to be written, is 'inevitable' but also 'abstract'; it cannot affect anything. Nevertheless even to *be*, in blackness and silence, must be embraced as a destiny that has meaning. Finally (and in the last stanza we reach the poem's most difficult passage) it may happen that some fragments of the poet's work and personality may come to light afterwards, as Mandelstam's did: in which case the 'eyes' of the poet, his organs of perception, become as far above human injustice as stars or planets; he becomes part of the order of nature rather than of man; his voice is 'echoless' because it is now beyond answering, just as it was in the 'unresonant' cell; but natural forces, too, affect our lives.

C. Day Lewis, b. 1904; educated at Sherborne School and Oxford. A prolific poet, translator, anthologist; Professor of Poetry, Oxford, 1951–6; Poet Laureate from 1968 until his death in 1972.

Louis MacNeice, b. Belfast 1907, son of a bishop. Educated at Marlborough and Oxford. Lecturer in Classics at Birmingham University 1930–6; Lecturer in Greek at Bedford College, London, 1936–40; joined the BBC as feature-writer and drama producer (radio) in 1940 and worked mainly for them for the rest of his life, apart from a spell as Director of the British Institute, Athens, in 1950.

Off-hand, unsentimental but deeply compassionate, MacNeice is one of the century's finest poets.

'Visitations VI': Being a poet is not a profession but a condition; having accepted (with no choice) the destiny of being a servant of the Muse – that destiny that is a 'doom and

153

heirloom' - one is always listening for her whispered instructions. MacNeice's view of the poet was that he was not a unique kind of person but a specially endowed version of the ordinary intelligent man; every human being has, constantly or intermittently, a sense of immortality (conveyed beautifully by the image of the soul 'untold light years inside him') and the python/lion/dove image of the last stanza applies to every human life; but the poet exteriorizes these feelings for us through his 'birthright and burden'.

Edwin Morgan, b. Glasgow 1920. Educated locally and at Glasgow University. RAMC 1940-6. Since then, has worked at Glasgow University where he is now Reader in English. Much original work; has translated from languages as varied as Anglo-Saxon, Italian, Russian, Hungarian.

John Ormond, b. near Swansea 1923. Educated locally and at University College, Swansea. Staff writer on *Picture Post* 1945-7; sub-editor *South Wales Evening Post* 1949-55, then joined BBC Television first as news editor, latterly as documentary film-maker.

Brian Patten, b. Liverpool 1946. Educated locally. Has won the Eric Gregory Award for poetry.
Patten's poems come directly out of contemporary urban life as lived by the young. He writes, as his generation usually read, as if there were no literary tradition and everything were being said for the first time; yet his poem in memory of Wilfred Owen takes as its starting-point the last two words of one of Owen's finest poems, 'Strange meeting'.

Alastair Reid, b. Wigtownshire, Scotland, 1926. Educated locally and at the University of St Andrews. Royal Navy, 1943-6. Lives mostly abroad, especially in Spanish-speaking countries, and has done notable work as a translator of Neruda, Borges, etc. Staff writer and correspondent for the *New Yorker* since 1959.

J. Burns Singer, b. New York, 1928, of Polish-Jewish-Irish parentage; was taken to Scotland at the age of four and educated there. Was trained, and worked, as a marine biologist; later, moved to London and engaged mainly in literary work. Died in 1964.

Stevie Smith, b. Hull 1909; as a child, moved with her family to Palmers Green, North London, and was educated there. She lived the rest of her life in Palmers Green, her last few years devoted to the care of a very old, bedridden aunt.

Stevie Smith wrote a successful novel in the 1930s, *Novel on Yellow Paper*, but she did not come into her own as a poet until the 1950s, when her work began to reach an increasingly wide audience; this fame was officially recognized by the award in 1969 of the Queen's Medal for Poetry. She died in 1971.

The name 'Hopdance' in *Mrs Blow and her Animals* is probably a reminiscence of the ravings of Edgar in *King Lear* III vi: 'Hopdance cries in Tom's belly for two white herring.'

Anne Stevenson, b. Cambridge 1933. Educated in England and America. Has worked as a schoolteacher, and as advertising manager for a publishing firm; various academic posts; Fellow in Creative Writing, University of Dundee, 1972-3. Lives in Oxford.

Dylan Thomas, b. Swansea 1914. Made a reputation as a poet ('the Rimbaud of Cwmdonkin Drive') before he was 20. Moved to London 1934; free-lance writer, broadcaster; famous for his readings on the radio and latterly on the lecture circuit; died in New York 1954.

Thomas in his later years remarked, 'I used to be arrogant and lost; now I'm humble and found.' He earned money as a star of the lecture circuit, but 'Lament' shows him ironically clear-sighted about himself as one of the 'dollar-mad nightingales' (his own phrase), a campus hero, perpetually surrounded by strangers, 'dying of welcome'.

D. M. Thomas, b. Redruth, Cornwall, 1935. Educated locally and at Oxford. Senior Lecturer in English at Hereford College of Education, 1963-78.

D. M. Thomas writes: 'My poetry does not move far from the great twin themes of love and death. Early poems (see *Penguin*

155

Modern Poets, 11) use science fiction themes as images of desire and separation. More recently, my most obsessive themes have been sexuality, family deaths and a search for lost roots in the brimming landscape of West Cornwall' (*Contemporary Poets*, ed. Vinson and Kirkpatrick, 1975).

'Stone' is a meditation on a poet's imaginative journey through life; D.M. Thomas himself has, I think, reached stage 2, which is why this poem itself is 'exasperated, warm, teasing, observant, tender'. The last stanza describes the ultimate state of achievement, when the poet in old age has thought himself into so deep a relationship with the world and with language that he can write as bare and unadorned a style as Milton did in *Samson Agonistes;* when he can choose very simple subjects – as Pablo Neruda wrote a poem about salt and another about a pair of socks – and say things, within that framework, which are bedrock truths.

R. S. Thomas, b. Cardiff 1912. Educated at the University of Wales. Ordained 1931. Is Vicar of St Hywyn, Aberdaron, Gwynedd.

Rosemary Tonks, b. London. Has lived in West Africa and Pakistan. Has written fresh, observant, witty novels as well as poetry.

She comments, 'I have developed a visionary modern lyric, and have had an idiom in which I can write lyrically, colloquially and dramatically. My subject is city life, with its sofas, hotel corridors, cinemas, underworlds, cardboard suit-cases, self-willed buses, banknotes, soapy bathrooms, news-paper-filled parks, and its anguish, its enraged excitement, its great lonely joys.' (*Contemporary Poets*, ed. Vinson and Kirkpatrick, 1975).

Rosemary Tonks, as her statement indicates, writes a poetry of mood, whose object is to convey the essence of metropolitan life as it is lived by clever people, alive to its endless variety and its frantic juxtapositions. If this or that detail in the poems is hard to capture in a paraphrase, put it back into the context of this mood and then the sometimes *outré* imagery, the comical exasperations, the associative leaps, all contribute powerfully to that mood.

Many modern poets, obviously, have lived in big cities, and to capture their bewildering and inciting atmosphere has been part of the effort of their work; one thinks of Guillaume Apollinaire, or of the Portuguese poet Fernando Pessoa, who says (as translated by Jonathan Griffin):

Daily multitudes of the streets, neither gay nor sad,
Multicoloured anonymous river in which I can bathe at will!
Ah, the complex lives of it all, the things there inside the houses!
Ah, to know how all of them live, their money troubles,
The domestic quarrels, the unsuspected debaucheries,
The thoughts that each one has by himself in his own room
And the gestures he makes when nobody can see!
Not knowing all this is to be totally ignorant - O rage,
O rage that like a fever and a rutting and a hunger
Gives me a drawn face and sometimes sets my hands twitching
Into absurd clenchings right in the middle of the people
In the streets full of encounters!

That, it seems to me, is the mood of Miss Tonks's poetry.

John Wain, b. Stoke-on-Trent, Staffordshire, 1925. Educated locally and at Oxford (where, at St John's, contemporaries included Philip Larkin and Kingsley Amis). Poet, novelist, short story writer, dramatist, biographer, autobiographer, literary and social critic; Professor of Poetry, Oxford University, 1973-8.

Wildtrack (1965) is a book-length poem on the subject - broadly - of those things that unite human beings rather than divide them. This section meditates on the sexual relation of man and woman; the Book of Genesis tells us that God fashioned Eve out of one of Adam's ribs, taken from his side while he slept. Jeanne Duval was the mulatto mistress of the poet Charles Baudelaire.

Derek Walcott, b. St Lucia, West Indies, 1930. Educated locally and at the University of the West Indies, Kingston, Jamaica. Has been university teacher and feature writer; now lives in Trinidad and is the Founding Director of the Trinidad Theatre Workshop; has had plays produced in London, notably at the Royal Court.

'Missing the sea': Like Rosemary Tonks's poems about

metropolitan life, this poem sets out to capture a mood: what it is like for someone accustomed (in the Caribbean, in this case) to the colossal and all-pervading physical presence of the sea to find himself removed from that presence. The house seems to lack a presence, even a dimension, so that the reflections one sees in mirrors seem curiously empty though one knows in fact they are perfectly complete. This emptiness pervades everything, even the linen-cupboards; when people die they go away from those who loved them, leaving their lives (the survivors' lives, that is) empty and unoccupied, as these folded clothes seem now to the poet; missing the sea, he has a continual sense that something is lacking, and these images convey it brilliantly.

Acknowledgements

For permission to reproduce copyright material the editor and publisher are grateful to the following:

Canongate Publishing Ltd and John Wolfers for 'Oddments, inklings, omens, moments', '1973', 'Growing, flying, happening', 'The O-filler' and 'My father, dying' by Alastair Reid from *Weathering*

George Allen & Unwin (Publishers) Ltd for 'Prose poem towards a definition of itself', 'Sleep now', 'Party piece' and 'What you should do each morning' by Brian Patten from *Little Johnny's Confession*

Faber & Faber Ltd for 'Visitations VI' and 'Hold-up' by Louis MacNeice from *The Collected Poems of Louis MacNeice;* 'Digging' from *Death of a Naturalist*, 'The Tollund man', 'Augury' and 'Mother of the groom' from *Wintering Out* and 'A constable calls' from *North*, all by Seamus Heaney; 'Verses for the 60th birthday of Thomas Stearns Eliot' from *News of the World* and 'Bleeding a stone is walking by the sea' from *A Vision of Beasts and Gods*, both by George Barker; 'Nemea' and 'Education of a cloud' by Lawrence Durrell from *Collected Poems;* 'Self's the man', 'Days', 'An Arundel tomb' and 'Reference back' from *The Whitsun Weddings* and 'Going, going' and 'The Explosion' from *High Windows*, both by Philip Larkin; 'I leave this at your ear' and 'The Don Brown Route' by W. S. Graham from *Malcolm Mooney's Land;* 'Witches', 'To paint a water lily' and 'Snowdrop' from *Lupercal* and 'Music on the moon' from *The Earth-Owl and other Moon People*, both by Ted Hughes; 'Moon landing' and 'Talking to mice' from *Epistle to a Godson*, 'Address to the beasts' and 'Thank you, fog' from *Thank You, Fog* and 'The shield of Achilles' from *The Shield of Achilles*, all by W. H. Auden; 'Considering the snail' from *My Sad Captains* and 'Mandrakes' from *Jack Straw's Castle*, both by Thom Gunn

Anvil Press Poetry for 'The tractor in spring', 'New Year's Eve poem 1965', 'For poets in prison without trial' and 'For Peter and Margaret' by Peter Levi from *Collected Poems*

Martin Secker & Warburg Ltd for 'Stone' and 'Lorca' by D. M. Thomas from *The Honeymoon Voyage*

Oxford University Press for 'On the cliff', 'Druid's circle', 'Manhood and youth' and 'The gamekeeper's dotage' by Tony Connor from *Kon in Spring Time* © Oxford University Press 1978; Oxford University Press and David Higham Associates Ltd for 'Song of the death-watch beetle', 'Address not known' and 'To the mermaid at Zennor' by John Heath-Stubbs from *Selected Poems*; Oxford University Press for 'Resurrection' by Anne Stevenson from *Enough of Green* © Anne Stevenson 1977; Oxford University Press for 'The piano tuner' by John Ormond from *Definition of a Waterfall* © John Ormond 1973

Christopher Davies (Publishers) Ltd for 'Cathedral builders', 'Definition of a waterfall' and 'At his father's grave' by John Ormond from *Requiem and Celebration;* 'Spirit level' by Anthony Conran from *Spirit Level*

Carcanet Press Ltd for 'Rembrandt's late self-portraits' and 'Elegy for W. H. Auden' by Elizabeth Jennings from *Growing Points;*

159

'Words made of water' by J. Burns Singer from *Collected Poems*; 'The first men on Mercury' by Edwin Morgan from *From Glasgow to Saturn*; 'Weeding' by Michael Hamburger from *Real Estate*

Allen Lane and James MacGibbon (executor) for 'The commuted sentence' and 'Mrs Blow and her animals' by Stevie Smith from *Collected Poems of Stevie Smith*

Macmillan Publishers Ltd for two extracts from *Wildtrack*, 'Anecdote of 2 a.m.' and 'Au Jardin des Plantes', from *Weep Before God* and 'Juliet and her nurse' from *Professing Poetry*, all by John Wain; Macmillan Publishers Ltd and David Higham Associates Ltd for 'Angel hill', 'On being asked to write a school hymn' and 'Who?' by Charles Causley from *Collected Poems*

Hutchinson & Co. (Publishers) Ltd and Anthony Sheil Associates Ltd for 'No more Mozart', 'Odd' and 'Haloes' by Dannie Abse from *Collected Poems 1948-1976*

Encounter for 'Letter from Leningrad' by Clives James

Jonathan Cape Ltd for 'Statues', 'Coral' and 'Missing the sea' from *The Castaway* and 'Dark August', 'Endings', 'Love after love' and 'Earth' from *Sea Grapes*, both by Derek Walcott; Jonathan Cape Ltd and the Executors of the Estate of C. Day Lewis for 'Walking away' from *The Gate*

J. M. Dent & Sons Ltd and the Trustees for the Copyrights of the late Dylan Thomas for 'Lament' by Dylan Thomas from *Collected Poems*

The Bodley Head and Richard Scott Simon Ltd for 'The sofas, fogs and cinemas' and 'Song of the October wind' by Rosemary Tonks from *The Iliad of Broken Sentences*

Chatto & Windus Ltd and Bolt & Watson Ltd for 'A common interest' by D. J. Enright from *Sad Ires and Others*

Cassell Ltd and A. P. Watt & Son for 'Testament', 'She tells her love' and 'To be called a bear' by Robert Graves from *Collected Poems*

The Marvell Press for 'Reasons for attendance' and 'Maiden name' by Philip Larkin from *The Less Deceived*

Rupert Hart-Davis Ltd/Granada Publishing Ltd for 'Kneeling' and 'The moor' by R. S. Thomas from *Selected Poems*

John Murray (Publishers) Ltd for 'Before the anaesthetic' and 'Hertfordshire' by John Betjeman from *Collected Poems*

André Deutsch Ltd for 'Merlin' from *Somewhere is such a kingdom* and 'Three baroque meditations' from *King Log*, both by Geoffrey Hill

The Hogarth Press Ltd for 'Tinkers' by George Mackay Brown from *Poems New and Selected*

Dolmen Press Ltd for 'The laundress' by Thomas Kinsella from *Selected Poems 1956-68*

Paul Elek Ltd for 'The journey' by D. M. Thomas from *Love and Other Deaths*

Routledge & Kegan Paul Ltd and Bolt & Watson Ltd for 'Children, beggars and schoolteachers' by D. J. Enright from *The Laughing Hyena*